SAINT FRANCIS
Of The Seven Seas

ST. FRANCIS

OF THE SEVEN SEAS

by ALBERT J. NEVINS, M. M.

Illustrated by LEO MANSO

Vision Books, *Farrar, Straus and Cudahy, New York*

Nihil obstat
JOHN M. A. FEARNS, S. T. D.
Censor Librorum

Imprimatur
✠ FRANCIS CARDINAL SPELLMAN
Archbishop of New York

Table of Contents

SAINT FRANCIS
Of The Seven Seas

Chapter 1

THE WEDDING

Francis stood on the topmost tower of Castle Xavier. By raising himself up on his toes, he could peer out over the stone walls around the tower and see the ground below. The sun was just rising over the steep hills near the castle, and the valleys were still filled with early morning mist. But already Francis saw a crowd of visitors trooping up the road that led to the castle drawbridge. So many people were coming to his sister's wedding.

Because it was Anna's wedding day, everyone in the family had risen very early. Castle Xavier was filled with many guests, and there was a great deal of talking and running about. After a quick breakfast, Francis had managed to escape unnoticed and climb the winding stone staircase to the top of one of the castle's towers.

The view from the tower was wonderful. Francis looked out over a wild, beautiful country of steep hills, dark woods, and swift streams. To the north lay a ragged chain of mountains, and beyond them the country of France. Francis let his glance drift closer to home. On near-by slopes he saw the ever-present shepherds with their sheep.

Francis walked to the opposite side of the tower and once again raised himself up on his toes. From this spot he looked down on the winding and fast-flowing Aragon River. He saw that some men who lived on his father's lands had poled a large raft of logs to shore. They were paying their tolls to a man who worked for his father. A little farther down the Aragon River, Francis saw the roof of the mill which was partly owned by his mother.

From the tower he could also see much of the Castle Xavier itself. Below were the moat, the drawbridge, and the other towers. Close to the castle was the small chapel where he and his family went to Mass every morning. Next to the chapel was the stone house where the three chaplains lived. One of these chaplains, Don Martin, had baptized Francis, and was his cousin.

"Francis!"

The small boy whirled around and saw his fifteen-year-old brother standing at the head of the stairs. Juan was strong and handsome, but now he was frowning darkly.

"I've been looking everywhere for you," he said. "You know mother doesn't want you up here alone. Get downstairs. It's almost time for the wedding."

Francis followed his brother down the narrow, steep stairway in silence. He knew Juan was angry at being made to look for him. But Francis knew too that Juan's anger never lasted long. He marched along at his brother's heels until at last they came to the main room of the castle.

"Ah, here are two of my sons!" Francis heard his father, Don Juan, exclaim as the boys entered the room. "Juan! Francis! Come here and meet our guests."

Francis and Juan walked over to where Don Juan was standing with some of his friends. Francis did not know his father very well, because Don Juan was away most of the time on the king's business. Don Juan was an adviser to the king of Navarre, the country in which Francis lived, and which now is part of Spain.

"My oldest son Miguel is outside," Don Juan remarked to his guests. "You will see him later. Juan is my second son, and Francis, my youngest child."

"You have two daughters, Don Juan, haven't you?" asked one of the guests.

"Yes," he replied, "Anna, who is to be married this morning. And Magdalena—"

"Isn't she a lady-in-waiting to Queen Isabella?" asked another man.

"She was," replied Don Juan. "She has now become a nun in a Poor Clare convent."

"A very strict life for a young girl," said one of the men.

"Magdalena is very holy," answered Don Juan simply.

"And these handsome sons of yours?" asked one of the visitors. "Are they going to become lawyers like you?"

"They must speak for themselves," replied Don Juan.

"Well, Juan, are you to be a lawyer?" the guest asked.

"No, sir!" said Juan. "The chaplains who teach us say I am not one for bookish study."

"Perhaps a bullfighter?" asked another visitor, half joking.

"Never!" declared Juan. "The secret of bullfighting is in keeping away from the bull. I do not wish to run away from things. I will be a soldier and serve the king."

"Good!" exclaimed the guest who had first spoken. "Your noble father has given his life in service to our king, and the king thinks most highly of him. You can find no better service."

"And you, Francis?" asked another man. "Will you be a soldier like your brother?"

"I do not know, sir," Francis replied shyly.

"Francis is only six years old," spoke up Don Juan. "He has plenty of time to decide what to do with his life."

"I am six years old," repeated Francis. "I was born April 7, 1506."

Don Juan and the guests laughed at the boy's serious reply. Under his dark skin, Francis blushed. He was glad when the chapel bell rang, calling everyone to the wedding. It was good not to have to answer any more questions.

Francis' mother, Doña Maria, was already in the chapel when he arrived. She was kneeling at prayer. Francis knelt, made the Sign of the Cross, and slid in alongside her. He glanced up at his mother's lovely and kind face. He thought that she was the most beautiful woman in the world.

Francis was too young to realize what great burdens his mother had to bear. Because his father was usually away from home, serving the king at his palace in Pamplona, Doña Maria had to take care of everything at Castle Xavier. She directed the work of the servants in the castle, and she supervised the men who collected rents on the Xavier lands and shepherds who guarded the family's flocks of sheep. But in spite of her thousand and one tasks, Doña Maria never forgot that her most important work was to raise her children as faithful subjects to God and the king. Francis was too young to understand all this, but he did know that his mother was good and kind, and his little heart was overflowing with love for her.

Like most small boys, he found it hard to

sit still in church and keep his mind on his prayers. He was happy when the wedding was over, and he could leave the dim chapel and go out into the sunlight again. While the guests talked with the bride and groom, Francis went into the courtyard.

Juan, Miguel, and some of the older boys who were visiting had started a game of *pelota* —a game that was a little like handball. Francis was too young to play, so he stood to one side and watched. The thought came into his head that it was a nice day to go fishing, but he dismissed it at once. With all the guests present, it would be rude to go away.

Suddenly, Francis heard the sound of a horse racing over the road. He ran to the courtyard gate just in time to see the rider turn his horse in a cloud of dust and come dashing across the drawbridge. The horseman was a soldier bearing the shield of King John of Navarre.

In the courtyard, the soldier flung himself off his horse, shouting, "Don Juan! Don Juan!"

As Francis hurried over, he saw his father hasten from the house. Since the horseman had been in such a big hurry, he must carry important news, Francis thought.

"King John of Navarre sends you this message: the king of Spain has declared war on France," said the messenger to Don Juan. "Since our country of Navarre lies between Spain and France, the king of Spain threatens to march his army through our land."

Don Juan's face became sad as he heard this news. After reading the letter which King John of Navarre had sent by messenger, he turned to the guests who had poured out of the house.

"I must leave at once," said Don Juan. "King John wishes me to tell the king of Spain that his soldiers must not march through our land. If they do, it will mean war."

"If the king of Spain ever gets his soldiers into Navarre," said one of the guests, "we will never get them out."

Don Juan told a servant to prepare a horse

at once for his journey. Then he went into the castle to change for the trip.

The wedding feast was ready by this time, so the family and the guests gathered in the dining hall and took their places at the long table. The company could not help but notice Don Juan's empty chair, and the absence of the lord of Castle Xavier removed much of the joy of the day. During the meal Don Juan came in to say good-by to his family and friends. Then Francis heard the hoofbeats as his father rode away.

It was several weeks before Don Juan returned to Castle Xavier. He rode in late one afternoon, tired and covered with dust.

"I must leave again at once," he told Doña Maria. "King John is waiting in Pamplona for my report. I only have time to wash, change my clothes, and get a bite to eat."

"Did you tell the king of Spain not to march through our land, father?" Miguel asked eagerly.

"I did," sighed Don Juan. "But he only

laughed at me. His troops are on their way into our country now. When they come, we will no longer be independent but will become part of his lands."

"We will never obey the king of Spain," declared Miguel angrily.

"A hundred of his soldiers cannot force a single one of us to obey," boasted Juan. "We will go with you and fight for King John of Navarre."

"No," replied Don Juan. "You must stay here with your mother. I must tell King John to flee, for we are not strong enough to win this war."

"But if the King flees, will you go with him?" asked Doña Maria worriedly.

"I have no choice," said Don Juan quietly. "I will flee with him. I must serve my king in bad times as well as good."

Don Juan hurried to his room, washed, changed his clothes, and then came down to the dining hall to eat before leaving. His wife and sons gathered around the table with him.

Francis was saddened at the concern of his mother and older brothers. But he did not realize what might happen because of his father's choice to remain with his king. Doña Maria and her older two sons knew what could happen. When the king of Spain was not able to catch King John and Don Juan, he might take out his anger on Castle Xavier. The Xavier family might lose its lands and possessions. But all of these things remained unsaid.

Doña Maria and her sons watched Don Juan jump on a fresh horse and ride across the drawbridge into the dusk. Because the Xaviers did not believe in giving way to their feelings, there were no sighs or tears.

As Don Juan disappeared in the darkness, the chapel bell rang out as it did every evening, calling all hearers to say the "Hail, Holy Queen."

"Let us go to chapel and pray for your father," said Doña Maria to her sons. "Our lives and fortunes are now in the hands of God."

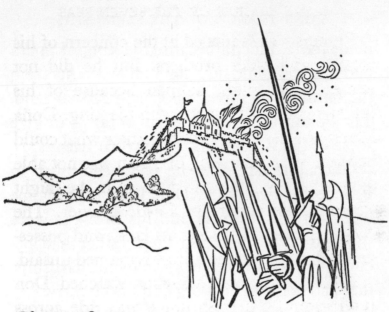

Chapter 2

A Ruined Castle

Francis did not see his father again for two years. During that time evil days fell upon Navarre and Castle Xavier. Navarre was made part of Spain. Spanish troops kept order in the cities and towns.

Doña Maria was hard put to make ends meet. With her husband away, she had to find a way to support the family. This task was made more difficult because the king of Spain had said she could no longer collect rents from the families who lived on Castle Xavier land. The Spanish king even went so far as to give some of the Xavier land to his own friends.

Then one day after he had been away in France for two years, Don Juan came home unexpectedly. Francis and his brothers were shocked to see how old their father had become. He was broken in spirit by the hardships that had come to his king and his country.

"I have not been well," Don Juan told his wife. "So I asked the king of Spain to allow me to return here."

Doña Maria knew that her husband was dying, but she did everything she could to make him well. Yet each day the lord of Xavier became weaker. Finally the chaplains at Castle Xavier were called to say the prayers for the dying.

Then one day Francis was told, "Your father has just died."

Francis was only nine years old. But the weeping of relatives and friends, the sad music of the Requiem Mass, and the deep sorrow of his mother, brothers, and sisters made a deep impression on the boy.

When King John heard of the death of his faithful friend, he sent some money to Doña Maria. But the king was himself poor and could not keep on helping her. Doña Maria sent a letter to the king of Spain, asking for aid. But he never answered.

In the next year, 1516, the king of Spain died. At once the people of Navarre revolted and tried to regain their freedom. But the Spanish soldiers soon stamped out the uprising, and the new ruler of Spain ordered that the people of Navarre should be punished.

One day, a troop of horsemen clattered up to Castle Xavier. Francis saw that they were Spanish soldiers, and he wondered what they wanted. His mother hurried out of the castle and went to the officer in charge.

"Are you Doña Maria?" asked the officer.

"Yes," replied Francis' mother. "What can I do for you?"

"You can do nothing for me," replied the

officer roughly. "As a punishment for the revolt in Navarre, every castle and fort is to be torn down. We have come here to see that this castle is destroyed."

"But no one here had anything to do with the revolt," said Doña Maria. "My husband died over a year ago."

"We have our orders," said the officer. "There is nothing I can do about them."

"But what will happen to us?" asked Doña Maria. "Must you tear down the homes of widows and fatherless children?"

"You should have thought of what would happen to you before you rebelled," declared the officer.

"I told you that we had nothing to do with the rebellion," repeated Doña Maria. "If you destroy our home, where are we to live?"

The leader of the soldiers called some of his officers aside while Francis watched anxiously. The soldiers spoke among themselves for a time. At last the leader returned to Doña Maria.

"We have come here to do justice," he declared, "not to harm widows and children. Most of your castle must be torn down. This is the order given to us. However, we shall leave a small part of it for you and your family to live in. I can do no more for you."

In the days that followed the soldiers and their helpers tore down Castle Xavier, stone by stone. Francis went into the hills each day to escape the sounds of destruction, the sorrow of his mother, and the flaming anger of his brothers. And each day when he returned home, more and more of the castle lay in ruins.

"The people of Navarre are very strange," one soldier said to another one evening. "I do not think that they will ever admit that their country now belongs to Spain."

"You are right," replied the other soldier. "They are a proud people who wish to live apart from the rest of the world. They refuse to speak Spanish, and they keep on speaking their own Basque language."

"Where did the Basques come from?" asked the first soldier.

"No one really knows," replied his friend.

"Certainly they are far removed from the Spanish, and they are unlike any other people of Europe. They have always resisted our efforts to teach them our way of life."

"Well, we have shown them that they cannot resist our army," said the first soldier with a laugh. "The more they try to fight, the more they will suffer."

"Yes, one must beat a dog to make him behave," agreed the other soldier. "The Basques may not speak the same language that we speak, but they can be made to understand the power of the sword. Every time they rebel, we will beat them down. Some day we will break their spirit."

The soldiers' words made a strong impression on Francis. He thought about them many times. The Spanish army was large and rich and strong, while Navarre had only a handful of troops. The people of Navarre might rebel, but in the end the great strength of Spain would win. Francis mentioned these thoughts to his brothers one day.

[28]

"You speak like a fool!" said Miguel angrily. "The Spanish understand only one language, the language of the sword. That is the only language that will regain our freedom."

"You read too many books," added Juan. "Your head is filled with silly ideas."

"But what has fighting gained for us?" asked Francis. "You think fighting is the answer to everything. But look at what is happening to our home."

"The Spanish dogs will pay for every stone they knock down," promised Juan. "Navarre will be free again."

"There must be another way," Francis said. "Our father did not believe in war. He served the king with his learning."

"You stay with your books," ordered Miguel with scorn in his voice. "We who are men will do the fighting."

This was the beginning of many disagreements and fights between the brothers. Juan and Miguel hated the Spanish. They teased and mocked their little brother for his peaceful ideas. If Francis had had a weak will, he would have given up his own beliefs. But he was as strong as his brothers. He felt that more warfare would mean more suffering. The family fortune could be regained only by peaceful means.

At last the soldiers finished their task and departed from the ruins of Castle Xavier. They left behind them a pile of wreckage. The great wooden doors of the castle had been burned out. The drawbridge had been chopped down, and the moat filled with rocks and earth. The outer walls and the watchtowers had been knocked down. In the midst of these ruins stood the small part of the castle which the soldiers had left for the widow and her family. They had also spared the chapel.

Not long after the soldiers had departed, Francis noticed that Miguel and Juan were slipping away from home at night. Usually they were home again by morning, but sometimes they would be gone for several days. Neither brother talked about the nighttime adventures, and for a long time Francis wondered where they went.

Then one day he heard about the guerrilla bands—rebels who hid in mountain forests and caves, and who attacked the Spanish soldiers when they were least expecting attack. When Francis heard about these guerrillas, he then knew what Miguel and Juan were doing when they were away from home. He was more certain than ever that his brothers were making a mistake, and he studied harder than ever with his chaplain teachers.

When Francis was fifteen, a civil war broke out in Spain, and most of the Spanish soldiers were hurriedly called home from Navarre. The people of Navarre thought that this was their chance to win back their freedom. They rose in revolt.

Miguel and Juan believed that the time had come when they could throw off the rule of Spain. They hurriedly gathered their followers and joined the army of Navarre which was marching on the city of Pamplona where a few

Spanish troops remained. The Spanish commander, seeing that he was outnumbered, decided to give up the city. Before doing so, he called a meeting of his officers and told them what he was going to do.

"Sir, if we do not fight to hold this city the people will say that we are cowards," said a young officer named Ignatius Loyola. "Never again will we be able to gain their respect. Spain depends upon us to hold Navarre. We alone can do it. I beg you to fight for the city."

Ignatius spoke with such force that his hearers clapped and shouted for him. Even the commander became filled with Ignatius' fire. Everyone agreed to make a fight for the city. For a long time the battle raged. Every time the army of Navarre tried to get over the city's walls, the Spanish troops hurled it back.

Then suddenly a cannon ball smashed through the wall at the place where Ignatius was fighting. The brave captain was directly in its path. One of his legs was crushed, the other badly injured. When Ignatius fell to the ground, his men lost heart. The commander then gave up the city.

The soldiers of Navarre treated Ignatius with kindness because they respected his bravery. His broken leg was set, and after two weeks of medical care he was placed in a stretcher and sent back to his own country. He was still very sick, and the doctors were not sure that he would ever walk again .

"Perhaps I was wrong," Francis told Don Martin, the priest who taught him. "I said that Navarre would never become free by means of the sword. Now we are free."

"I don't think you were wrong, Francis," the priest replied. "It doesn't matter who wins the first fight because only the final battle counts. Spain will soon send more troops here. Then I fear for your brothers."

Don Martin was right. As soon as the Spanish ruler heard about the fall of Pamplona, he sent his army into Navarre. In a battle near Pamplona, his troops defeated the men of Navarre and regained the city. The soldiers of Navarre were sent flying in every direction.

"This is the end of Navarre," Don Martin told Francis. "Spain will never make the same mistake again. Soon the young men of Navarre will be drafted for the Spanish army."

"But I do not want to be drafted," said Francis. "I would not like to be a soldier."

"Would you like to be a priest?" asked Don Martin. "I think you would make a good priest, Francis."

"Perhaps," the boy replied with a smile. "But I would not be satisfied to remain a priest for long. I would have to become a bishop or a cardinal."

"Not at all impossible," said Don Martin. "I am sure the bishop would be willing to make you a canon at the cathedral in Pamplona. That would be a start. You have a quick mind, and you enjoy studying, Francis. You would do well in a Church career."

"We will see," said Francis. "But I know I would rather enter the Church than the army."

"Is there any word of Miguel or Juan?" asked Don Martin.

"Miguel sent a message to my mother," replied Francis. "He and Juan are in the mountains with the guerrillas. He says that they are going to keep fighting until Navarre is free again."

"A foolish dream!" exclaimed Don Martin. "They would do better to come home here and help your mother. Things are not easy for her."

"Miguel and Juan have strong wills," said Francis.

"And you?" asked Don Martin. "What kind of a will have you?"

"I am equal to to either of them," answered Francis with a broad smile.

A few days later word reached the castle that in a guerrilla attack, Miguel had been captured. He had been taken to a dark prison in Pamplona where he was being held for execution. The news was a terrible blow to Doña Maria. She spend long hours in chapel praying that God would help her son. One day while she was at prayer, Francis hurried into the chapel.

"Mother! Miguel is safe!" exclaimed Francis. "A messenger has just arrived. Last night Miguel made a bold and daring escape from his prison. He is now hidden in the mountains with Juan."

Doña Maria blessed herself and hurried out of the chapel behind her son. Quickly she questioned the messenger.

He said, "Miguel and Juan are on their way to a fort where other soldiers of Navarre are gathered. This fort is so strong that no Spanish force will ever capture it."

A few days later, word reached Castle Xavier that Spain had sent a large body of troops to attack the fort. But despite many attacks, the Spanish soldiers were not able to get into the fort. Weeks passed into months, and months into years, but still Miguel, Juan, and the other young soldiers from Navarre held out.

While his two brothers were busy with adventure, Francis fretted at Castle Xavier. He felt that he had gone as far with his studies at home as he could. He wanted to go to Paris, which was then the center of learning. But he could not go and leave his mother alone. The only way for him to get away was for his brothers to be pardoned so that they could return to Navarre. But there seemed to be little chance of that happening. Francis felt trapped.

During these years Francis had grown into a strong and handsome young man. He was fond of books but equally fond of sports. His charm drew others to him. He had the typical Basque desire to keep his feelings to himself, but he also had a polite, friendly manner that pleased everyone who knew him.

Often when Francis was daydreaming or making plans for his future, his dark face would light up with a broad smile. He had great ambitions, and he believed that by his own powers he could gain these ambitions. But not at Castle Xavier! He needed to study in

Paris. But he could not leave the castle unless by some miracle his brothers returned home.

Then in 1524 the miracle happened. The Spanish ruler decided that it was too expensive to keep up the attacks on the Navarrese fort. He offered to pardon the men if they would surrender. Miguel and Juan finally accepted the terms and were allowed to return home to Castle Xavier.

Francis lost no time in talking over his plans with Miguel who had become the head of the family following Don Juan's death.

"Now that you are home, and mother will not be left alone, I want to go ahead with my studies in Paris," Francis told his brother.

"Impossible," replied Miguel. "War has left us poor. There is no money for such luxuries."

"Education is no luxury!" exclaimed Francis hotly. "It is war that made us poor. By learning I can obtain a far higher position than you ever could win with your sword."

"You'll get no money from me," said Miguel angrily. "If you value learning so highly, use it to find a way to go to Paris."

Francis flushed with anger of his own. It seemed as if in a moment the two brothers would be settling their disagreement with force. It was Doña Maria who came to the rescue of her youngest child. She knew what a strong ambition burned in Francis.

"I still have a small share in a mill," she said. "It is not much but it will pay for Francis' education."

Miguel began to object, but his mother silenced him. "The money from the mill is my own. I can do with it what I will," she declared. "Francis will go to Paris."

Thus in September, 1525, Francis Xavier set out from the castle for a five-hundred-mile walk to Paris. Before him lay hard travel over steep mountains, through thick forests, and along dangerous roads. With the dreams of youth singing in his heart, he saw the world opening up to him. Ahead lay the pleasures and adventures of Paris—all of them would soon be his. He was then nineteen years old.

Chapter 3

COLLEGE DAYS

The University of Paris was a tangle of some fifty buildings huddled along the south bank of the Seine River. Most of the schools, rickety and dark, were built on narrow, dirty streets. Stores and rooming houses were crowded around the school buildings. The University of Paris had lost some of its old greatness and beauty, but it was still the most important place of learning in the world. It attracted students from as far away as Arabia and Persia.

Francis found himself in the largest city he had ever seen. Paris at that time was not the beautiful city of parks and statues and wide streets that it is today, but, even so, the size of the city and its strange sights and smells and noises dazzled the country boy who was away from home for the first time.

"I want only the best school," Francis had told his cousin and teacher, Don Martin, before leaving Navarre.

"St. Barbara's College is the best college in the University of Paris," Don Martin had replied.

Francis was thinking of his teacher's words as he brushed past the beggars and tradesmen who thronged the narrow streets of Paris.

"Can you direct me to the College of St. Barbara?" Francis asked a passing priest.

"Do you see those spires in the distance?" asked the priest in return. "That is the Church of St. Genevieve. It is on the edge of the Latin Quarter where you wish to go."

"Latin Quarter?" questioned Francis.

"Yes, it is the part of Paris where you will find the colleges," explained the priest. "It is called the Latin Quarter because the students talk to each other in Latin there. Keep walking along this street until you come to the walls of the old city, and pass through the Gate of St. James. Then walk to the Street of the Dogs. There you will see your college."

Francis followed the directions into the Latin Quarter and at last found the College of St. Barbara, a high, rambling building that went up one street, down a second and around again a third. He located the office of the headmaster, chose his courses, and paid his fees as a boarding student.

"I have given you a room with a student named Peter Fabre," the master told Francis. "Take your belongings up there, and then go to a tailor shop and buy the hat and gown you must wear to your classes."

Francis left his belongings in his room, bought the hat and long black gown, and was hardly back in his room when older students began to drop around. Francis did not know it, but these older students had heard that he came from a rich family, and they wanted to help him spend his money. They invited him to join them at some of the gay places of Paris.

Francis' first freedom went to his head. He played more than he studied. He was always on the go. Street carnivals, songfests, parties, boxing matches—all were sources of pleasure for the young nobleman from Navarre.

"You ought to break away from your books," Francis said to his roommate, Peter Fabre, one day. "You're missing all the fun."

"What are you doing today, Francis?" Peter asked.

"I'm going up to the Isle St. Louis," Francis replied. "There are contests in sports up there. I've entered the high jump."

"Some of the students say you are very good at high jumping," remarked Peter.

"There is no one around who is better,"

Francis replied with a broad smile. "Since I've started taking part in these contests, I've made more and more friends. And with new friends come new invitations to parties. Well, I must be off. Oh, Peter—"

"Yes?"

"I've ordered some more new clothes," said Francis. "If the boy should bring them around, take them from him, will you? Tell him that I'll stop at the tailor shop in a day or so and pay my bill. Don't study too late."

Francis enjoyed his free time much more than his class time, for college life in those days was very strict. Students got up at four o'clock in the morning, said their prayers, and went off to their classes with their books, inkpots and candles. At five o'clock the first class began. The students sat on the floor of a cold, drafty classroom. In winter, straw was spread over the floor so that it would be a little more comfortable. After the first class, the students went to Mass. This was followed by breakfast —a roll and a cup of water.

Classes began again at eight o'clock and

lasted until eleven. Then came dinner—a bit of fish or an egg with vegetable stew and a cup of wine. After dinner each boy studied alone until three o'clock when classes began again for two more hours. The day ended with supper, more study, and bed at nine o'clock. This was supposed to be the schedule, but many students skipped classes and spent the night on parties.

Classes themselves were far from interesting. Many of the classrooms at St. Barbara's College were crowded. Students came and went as they pleased, for attendance at classes was not marked down. A student could stay at college as long as he had money to pay the fees. It was up to him to decide when he wanted to take the examination for his graduation. There was no one to check up on his progress but himself.

The teacher kept order with a big stick. Many people said that the stick was a better teacher than the professor himself. The teacher would beat a student for falling asleep or talking. Often classes were interrupted by the howls of a student getting a beating in another room. The teacher's voice could be heard shouting in anger, there would be a swish of the stick, then a cry of pain from the student. Even students who were grown men were beaten if they did not behave.

"If that is the way the teachers are going to treat us," Francis declared to his roommate, "I'll get away with everything I can. I'll enjoy myself, and do no more studying than is necessary."

"Your tailor was here again," Peter remarked.

"What did he want?" asked Francis.

"His money," Peter replied.

"He's always bothering me for money," said Francis in a hurt tone of voice. "I've a good mind to take my business elsewhere. After all, I'm the best customer he has."

"Another thing," Peter went on. "I don't like that fellow you hired as your servant. I caught him snooping around in my box of clothes."

"Oh, he is harmless," Francis replied with

a wave of his hand. "After all a man in my position must have a servant. If I didn't have him around, some of the students would get a false idea of the nobility of Navarre."

"I had the idea that your family had come on hard times," Peter said.

"For the moment," Francis admitted. "But that is no reason for lowering one's way of living. But let's not talk about money. You know how I despise such talk. The nobly born must nobly live."

Francis' manner of life caused him to write home often for more and more money. Miguel, knowing how hard it was for the family to keep Francis in Paris, grew angry and wanted to order him home. First, however, the older brother consulted other members of the family.

Francis' sister, Magdalena, a holy nun, wrote to Miguel: "Do all you can to help the studies of our brother for I feel sure that he will become a great servant of God and pillar of the Church."

Miguel followed her advice and allowed

Francis to remain in Paris. But few people seeing the gay, happy life of the young man would have believed that Magdalena was right about her brother. There was no sign that Francis would become even a worth while man, not to mention a saint.

Francis' roommate, Peter Fabre, lived quite differently from him. Peter came from a peasant family of western France. As a boy minding sheep, he used to weep alone and unseen because he could not go to school.

His mother and father knew his desire, so they scraped and saved to get enough money together to send their son to Paris. The priest of Peter's village, a kind and generous man, taught Peter Latin and other subjects for nine years so that the boy would be prepared to go to college.

Peter and Francis did not become friends quickly. Their backgrounds were too different. They had nothing in common. At first Francis looked down on the unmannered former shepherd and even disliked being in the same room with him. Francis had a quick mind, and he did not have to work hard to learn. He studied as little as he could. Peter, on the other hand, had to work hard to learn. By slow and steady plodding he was making himself into a scholar. Peter thought Francis was silly to spend so much time playing, while Francis thought Peter was foolish to study so hard.

Yet Francis had a charm and politeness that appealed to Peter. Francis' life of castles and kings and wealth could not help but impress this shepherd boy who had known only work and poverty. So in many ways, Peter looked up to Francis. He often wondered what would happen if Francis put to good use the talents God had given him.

Peter was not without his own charm. He had an open friendliness that came from his country boyhood. Try as he might, Francis couldn't help liking his roommate. Nor could he help respecting Peter. Francis knew that he should study more and play less. Being fair by nature he had to admit to himself that Peter was doing the better thing—but it was harder, and Francis wasn't ready for anything hard just yet.

In one thing Peter was a bit like Francis— he, too, was not sure where he was headed. One evening he said to Francis, "I don't know what kind of work I want to do. One day I plan to be a doctor, and on other days to become a lawyer or a school teacher or a priest."

Francis replied, "At least you have some ideas of what you might want to be. I am just drifting along with the tide—but I'm having a very good time while I drift," he added with a smile.

Neither Peter nor Francis knew when their friendship began. It grew slowly, becoming deeper and warmer with the passing days. It flowered as they talked of the future and came to understand the other better.

While Peter and Francis were enjoying their college days, the force that would shape their futures was fast approaching. It came in the form of a limping, middle-aged man driving before him a donkey loaded with books, a man at whom others laughed and poked fun. But this man was to change not only the lives of Peter Fabre and Francis Xavier, but also the lives of countless men and women in all parts of the world in times yet to come.

This man was Ignatius Loyola.

Chapter 4

THE LIMPING SOLDIER

At the age of thirty-three, Ignatius Loyola
arrived in Paris with his books, a donkey, and
twenty-five gold pieces. He found lodging in
a boarding house where many Spaniards lived,
and he gave his twenty-five gold pieces to one
of them for safekeeping. The fellow promptly
ran off with the money. Ignatius sold his
donkey, and when that money was used up, he

went to live in a poorhouse. He began classes at Montaigu College, and in his free time spoke to anyone who would listen about the love of God that burned in his heart.

"Have you heard about the limping Spaniard who is preaching in the streets?" Peter asked Francis one day.

"Everywhere I go I hear about him," Francis replied. "The whole University of Paris is laughing at the poor fool."

"Perhaps he is not such a fool," said Peter. "I understand that he used to be a very rich and brave officer. But after his leg was crushed in a battle, he turned from army service to the service of God. He seems to be sincere."

"Sincere!" snorted Francis in his most grand manner. "He's crazy! A gentleman who has become a beggar! A fool spreading foolish ideas! He should mind his own business. I want nothing to do with him."

"You aren't afraid of him, are you?" teased Peter.

"Afraid of Ignatius Loyola!" Francis laughed. "Do you know where he got his limp? In the battle of Pamplona fighting on the side of our enemies. Perhaps one of my own brothers fired the cannon ball that crippled him."

Because the College of St. Barbara was directly across the street from Montaigu College attended by Ignatius, Francis often saw him on his way to or from school. However, Francis would not speak to him and tried to keep from crossing paths with him.

One night, the most promising student at St. Barbara's College disappeared along with two classmates. The next day it was learned that the three students had become disciples of Ignatius. They had gone to live with him in the poorhouse. The students at St. Barbara's were very angry. They marched on the poorhouse with clubs and swords, hurling curses and threats at Ignatius.

"We do not wish to return to the college with you," the three converts said to their fellow students. "We have given up worldly pleasures. We wish to follow Ignatius Loyola."

The students stormed the building, discovered that Ignatius was not around, and dragged "the deserters" back to their college.

The next morning Ignatius told some of his friends, "I was once a soldier, and as a soldier I know that the best defense is to attack the source of the trouble. I am leaving Montaigu College and entering St. Barbara's College."

The students at the College of St. Barbara were outraged when Ignatius appeared among them.

But no one was as put out as Francis Xavier. The headmaster called Francis aside and told him that Ignatius would stay in the room with him and Peter Fabre.

"Loyola will have much work to do if he is to catch up with the students here," said the headmaster. "I shall expect you to help him with his studies."

Francis was filled with disgust at the news. He hurried to Peter and told him of their new roommate.

"You know I can't stand the fool," Francis said. "Be a good fellow, Peter, and teach him for me. You know more than I do anyway."

"I'll do it," Peter agreed. "Loyola may not be as bad as you think."

Thus a third bed was added to Francis Xavier's room, and Ignatius Loyola moved in. Francis stayed away from the room as much as he could, returning home only to sleep. Peter, however, found that Ignatius was quite different from what he had expected. Before long Peter was telling the older man his problems and asking for advice.

Ignatius soon brought peace into the heart of the young student. After he and Peter had become close friends, he told Peter about the turning point of his life.

It had happened while Ignatius was recovering from an operation on the leg that was crushed at the battle of Pamplona. He had asked for some books and had been given some stories about saints and the life of Christ. He did not wish to read spiritual books, but because there was nothing else around, he began to read them to take his mind off his painful leg.

The books changed Ignatius' life. He found

a new goal. He would no longer be the champion of a royal lady and do battle for her. He would become the champion of the Mother of God and fight under the banner of Christ. And so one night he arose from his bed and knelt down in a corner of his room before a picture of the Blessed Mother.

"If others can serve you, dear Lady," he whispered, "so can I. From now on my whole life will be devoted to your service."

When Ignatius was well, he left his home. Meeting a beggar, he exchanged his handsome clothes for a beggar's rags. He lived in a cave, keeping himself alive by begging stale bits of bread. During his long days of prayer and fasting, he would jot down notes for a book he was to call *Spiritual Exercises*—a guidebook for those who wished to become saints.

Peter Fabre wished to become a saint and was happy to follow the lead of Ignatius. But Francis was not as easily won. In order to get away from the former soldier, Francis asked permission to live in a different room for a time. Francis made jokes about his strange roommate and laughed at his efforts to bring men to God.

Meanwhile, Francis and Peter finished college and won their degrees. Francis began teaching at one of the colleges, but he kept on living at Saint Barbara's. Because Francis was always in need of money, he began to tutor students in his free time. He was surprised when he learned that Ignatius had sent some of the students to him. He was even further surprised when from time to time Ignatius would lend him money.

Finally Ignatius did win Francis' friendship and trust. It happened during a seven month period in 1533 when Peter Fabre had gone home to visit his family. When Peter left, Francis still had no use for Ignatius, but upon Peter's return he found that Francis was one in mind and heart with the older man.

When Peter asked Francis how this had happened, the young nobleman explained, "Through my talks with Ignatius, I came to ask myself this question: 'What would it profit me to gain the whole world if I lose my own soul?' So I decided to save my soul by following Ignatius in the service of God."

With Francis Xavier, Ignatius had six fervent disciples. The little band met regularly, and, one by one, Ignatius taught them his spiritual exercises. At each meeting the men studied how they could better serve God. They planned to make a pilgrimage to the Holy Land, visiting the places where the Lord lived and died. They decided to take an oath to serve God faithfully.

Under Ignatius' guidance Peter Fabre had become a priest. One day after he had said Mass, the other members of the group knelt in prayer and made a vow to serve God.

After taking his vow, Francis went to a quiet place to pray and to think about God in the way Ignatius suggested in his book, *Spiritual Exercises*. Francis was now sorry that he had wasted so many years of his life in play.

To make up for the bad things he had done,

he fasted and tied his arms so tightly to his body that he was unable to move them. Soon Francis' arms started to swell around the tight cord—but he would not allow his friends to free him. In a few hours the swelling covered the cord. Then there was no way to cut it. His friends, full of sorrow for him, gave themselves to prayer, fearing that at least one of his arms would have to be cut off.

For two days of terrible pain, Francis prayed and did penance for his sins. All the time his arms became more and more discolored. All who saw him felt sure that blood poisoning had set in. Then at the end of the second day the ropes suddenly broke and his arms healed as if by a miracle.

Back at Saint Barbara's, Ignatius hung a picture of Jesus on the door of the room where he, Francis, and Peter lived. He did this to show that those in the room were trying to serve God. One of the students saw the picture and decided that it suggested a way to mock the three who were trying to lead holy lives.

Below the picture he wrote in big letters *Society of Jesus.*

Without knowing it, the scoffing student had given the name to the group that would become one of the greatest orders in the Catholic Church. The Society of Jesus! The smallest of small mustard seeds! Even Ignatius and his six disciples did not dream of the great work their order would do in times to come.

Chapter 5

FRANCIS BECOMES A PRIEST

After Francis had made his spiritual exercises, Ignatius said, "I must leave for Spain to raise the money for our pilgrimage. We shall travel by ship to the Holy Land from Venice, Italy, so I will meet you in Venice a year from now."

Therefore, in November 1536, Francis and his friends said good-by to Paris. Wearing cassocks and wide-brimmed hats, they started their long walk through France and Switzerland to Italy.

It rained all the way through France, and every day the travelers were soaked and chilled. Then the rain changed to snow. Each night they spent a few pennies to buy bits of food. They did not have enough money to hire a room, so they slept on the floors of inns and barns. It was a hard journey, but they were filled with a joy that comes to those that give themselves to God.

After two months of walking, starving, and freezing, the weary group reached Venice and found Ignatius waiting for them. He said that his trip to Spain had been successful. Then he gave them bad news. There would be no ships sailing to the Holy Land until June. And even then they could not be sure of getting passage, because war might break out with the Turks.

"In order that we have something to do while we wait," Ignatius told his followers, "I have arranged for us to work at two hospitals here in Venice, Saints John and Paul Hospital and the Incurable Hospital."

Francis started work at the hospital for incurable people. Many lepers were patients in this hospital. The work was not easy, and Francis who liked nice things had to fight with himself in order not to show his disgust at many of the terrible sights he saw.

He and his friends made beds, swept the floors, emptied and cleaned bedpans, kept the wards cleaned, and carried the bodies of the dead to graves. Day and night they cared for the sick with so much joy that they astonished the people living at the hospital.

It was in this hospital that Francis had his first close contact with a leper. This poor man was covered all over with great open sores out of which a foul-smelling liquid ran. One day as Francis was passing the leper, the man called out, "Ho, there! Please rub my back."

Francis went over to the man. When he saw the terrible sores and smelled the ugly odor, he felt that he was going to be sick and faint. He was filled with a horror that he might catch the disease. He wanted to run away quickly. But deciding to crush his feelings he scraped up some of the foul-smelling liquid with his fingers and swallowed it.

"Last night," Francis told another disciple the next day, "I dreamed that the leprosy of the sick man was caught in my throat. I could not get rid of it by coughing or other means."

After two months of work in the hospitals, Francis and his friends decided to go to Rome and beg the blessing of the Pope for their pilgrimage to the Holy Land. Because it was Lent, they chose not to carry any food, but to live by begging alone. It was a bad choice, because for three days of their trip they did not meet a single person. Moreover, it rained all the way, and they had to walk through mud and water that was waist deep. They were so hungry that they ate the seeds out of pine cones. They slept in barns or wet fields. It was a journey that none of them would ever forget.

At last the weary travelers reached Rome

and were admitted to see the Pope. He was so pleased with their learning and their holiness that he gave his blessing to the pilgrimage and presented them with some money for it. He also gave his permission for Francis and some of his friends to be ordained priests.

Happy, the group returned to Venice. Ignatius decided that the men who had been given permission to become priests should pray for forty days. Then they would be ordained. Francis and another disciple, Salmeron, found a deserted hut where they could pray and prepare themselves. They obtained their food by begging and spent the rest of the time in prayer.

On June 24, 1537, Francis Xavier was ordained to the priesthood. Shortly after he said his first Mass, he took sick and was removed to a hospital. For days he took turns shivering and burning with fever. As soon as he felt that his strength was returning, he left the hospital.

By this time war with the Turks had begun, and it was impossible to go to the Holy Land.

Therefore Ignatius sent his priests to work in different cities.

A year later when the group met again, they talked about forming themselves into a society with one of them elected as a head. After much talk and prayer, they drew up a set of rules and sent them to the Pope, asking his approval. In these rules they called themselves the Society of Jesus, and they said that they wished to be soldiers of God and to fight under the banner of the Cross. On September 27, 1540, the Pope gave his approval and the Society was born. Ignatius was elected head of the new society, which soon became known as the Jesuits.

While this was going on, a letter arrived for Ignatius from Paris. It was from one of the teachers at Saint Barbara's College. "The ruler of Portugal is interested in having missioners go to India," said the letter. "Would Ignatius be interested in sending some of his priests there?"

Ignatius wrote back that he was interested, because the new society would do missionary work both at home and in foreign lands. Letters went back and forth between Portugal and Ignatius. It was finally decided that two priests would be sent to India to begin the first mission—Father Rodriguez and Francis Xavier.

Francis hurried to repair his only pair of trousers. He threw a few bits of clothing into a small bag, along with two books—his breviary and a copy of parts of the New Testament. That was all he needed for the journey half way around the world!

Chapter 6

OFF TO THE INDIES

Francis Xavier stood at the rail on the high deck of the flagship *Santiago,* anchored near the docks of Lisbon, Portugal. Alongside of him was Doctor Saraiva, the ship's doctor. It was April 7, 1541.

"A happy day to start our journey, Father," said the doctor.

"It is a beautiful day," replied Francis.

"That's not what I meant. I heard the governor say that today is your birthday."

"Yes, my thirty-fifth," answered Francis.

"Are you happy that we are leaving Portugal?" asked the doctor.

"Yes," Francis replied. Then realizing that the answer might be misunderstood, he explained, "Portugal is lovely, and Lisbon is a wonderful city. But I came here to leave for India. I am glad that at last after almost a year of waiting I am able to start on the journey."

"But you did not spend the year in idleness," said Doctor Saraiva. "I have heard that the king was very impressed with the wonderful work you and Father Rodriguez did for the poor and for sinners."

"There is much work in Lisbon," agreed Francis. "That is why Father Rodriguez has remained behind. What is that wailing I hear over there on the docks?"

"The last boatload of sailors is coming out to our ship," said the doctor. "The wailing is from their wives, mothers, and sweethearts.

[72]

Those women know that many of their men will never return. A journey to India is no pleasure trip. We must face scurvy, cholera, tropical diseases, pirates, and storms. Many a man aboard the ship will not live through this journey."

"Have you made the trip before?" Francis asked the doctor.

"No, thank God!" he replied. "I go only because the governor is my friend. I have seen the records of these trips. Of every ten men who sail to India, four die before the goal is reached. One ship carrying eleven hundred men arrived in India with only two hundred still alive."

"What is the reason for so many deaths?" asked Francis.

"Look about you, Father!" said the doctor, gesturing about the ship. "There are a thousand men aboard. Only the governor, the captain, and a few important officers have cabins. The rest of us must live here on the open decks. We cannot escape the sun, nor is there any place to flee from the rain. Disease can spread among us like fire."

"Yes, I can see the dangers," agreed Francis.

"In the best of times we get one hot meal a day," the doctor went on. "We must eat with our fingers. When the weather is stormy, fires cannot be lighted, so there is no hot meal."

"Even so, we won't starve," said Francis. "I saw the sailors bringing plenty of food aboard."

"You saw salted beef and pork come aboard," said the doctor. "Each morning huge chunks of this meat will be put in tubs of salty water here on deck. Barefooted sailors will trample on it to make it tender. We also have rice, cheese, and salted fish for fast days. But what happens when we are becalmed in the tropics? Everything goes bad. In the steaming heat, even the most carefully salted meats begin to rot. Those parts of the ship above water begin to split apart. The deck is a red-hot oven. Men die of thirst. And then do you know what happens?"

"No," said Francis. "What?"

"The rains come—the cruel warm rains. Our clothing rots. Our skins become covered with boils. Your heart will be torn apart, Father, as you watch the poor, bloated bodies of the dead being dropped into the sea. Those women on shore know these things, and that is why they are wailing. We Portuguese explore and colonize, Father. But at what a high cost in pain and suffering!"

"We must trust in God," said Francis in a low voice. "There are souls waiting for us at the end of this journey. God's Son paid an even higher price to save them."

"I don't mean to alarm you with these stories, Father," said the doctor. "You will have a year aboard this ship to learn them at first hand. We will soon be underway."

There was a command from one of the officers. Some sailors scrambled aloft to the sails, and others began pulling in the anchor chain. The men started singing a religious chant.

Francis whispered a prayer that God would

bless the journey. Then the boat began moving slowly away from shore. Francis looked back to get his last glimpse of Europe. He saw Lisbon rising proudly on its seven steep hills. He recognized the broad public plaza with its sweeping steps at one end leading up to the royal palace. Slowly the ship moved farther away. The lovely Church of Jeronymos, where he had offered Mass, disappeared. Then only the tall tower of Belen stood out on the skyline. Finally that too was out of sight. Europe was behind him.

The *Santiago* made for the open sea. It was a big, bulky ship of a hundred tons, half as wide as it was long. Three masts rose from the decks, and at the top of each mast was a platform for the lookouts. Because of its heavy stern rudder, the boat was hard to steer, and in a storm there was always the danger it would capsize. The three sails were unfurled and catching the breeze. At top speed the boat moved along at about five miles an hour.

Darkness fell and Francis' first night

aboard the *Santiago* began. From the bow of the ship, someone started chanting the "Hail, Holy Queen." The prayer was taken up by a thousand voices. In the darkness Francis blessed himself and sang along with the others. When the prayer was finished, he went to find his place to sleep.

In the days that followed Francis went about the ship comforting and nursing the sick. He also spent much of his time talking to men about God and hearing confessions.

Francis, never a man to say much about himself, wrote to Ignatius of the trip. He said that he had been seasick for two weeks and that the *Santiago* had been becalmed for forty days. During this time some men died. He said that he was able to comfort them and give them the Sacraments.

"The hardships of the voyage were of such a kind," he added, "that but for God's sake I would not have faced them during a single day even if I were to be given the whole world."

Yet despite all his hard work, Francis could

not help everyone on the ship. Just after the ship reached the island of Mozambique off the coast of Africa, where it had to spend the winter, a young man suddenly died.

"Did he know Jesus Christ?" asked Francis when he heard of the death.

The dead man's fellow passengers replied that he did not. Francis was overcome with a great sorrow.

"Don't feel so sad," they told Francis. "You did not know him."

"That's what makes me sad," replied Francis. "If I had known him, I would have taught him. To think that I should have been on the same ship with him all those months and not told him of Christ!"

Mozambique was known as the "Portuguese graveyard." It was given this name because of the many sailors and travelers who died there. Francis did a great deal of work during the time he stayed at Mozambique. He worked so hard that he soon fell sick. The ship's doctor took him to his own house and put him to bed.

For three days Francis was unconscious. The doctor bled him nine times during this illness. Bleeding was thought to be a cure for sickness in those days. A vein was opened in the ill person's arm, and blood was allowed to run out, because it was believed that the disease would also leave with the blood.

As soon as Francis began to get better, he started visiting Mozambique's sick again. The doctor begged him to slow down if he did not wish to kill himself.

"At least wait until you are well again yourself," said the doctor.

"Perhaps, tomorrow," replied Francis. "Tonight I must take care of a poor fellow who is at death's door. When he is friendly with God, I will rest."

The next day the doctor visited the hospital and went to the little room where Francis lived. Francis had put the sick man in his own bed, and he lay alongside the bed on some boards. The doctor found Francis talking to the sailor, just as he had done throughout the night.

When the sailor died later that day, he was well prepared to meet God, having made his confession and received Holy Communion.

"The man's happy death caused the Father no end of happiness," the doctor remarked to a friend. "Indeed, Father Francis always looks happy, no matter how great his own sufferings may be."

In February, after six months at Mozambique, Francis set out once again for India—a good two month's journey away. Again he began his gentle and good works for those aboard who needed help. On this voyage he turned over his own bed to those who were sick. He slept in the hollow of the anchor chain, using the anchor itself as his pillow.

Finally on May 6, 1542, the boat carrying Francis Xavier reached India. It dropped anchor at the Portuguese colony of Goa. Francis Xavier was then thirty-six years old, but his face was drawn from the many illnesses he had suffered since he began working for God. His body was weakened because he refused to allow it rest. But he was doing the work of God, so he trusted God to give him the strength he needed. Francis had one driving rule: he would go the whole way for Christ. He would give every bit of strength in him.

So Francis stepped ashore, weak in body but strong in desire. His soul was aflame to tell all men about God. How many of them could he reach before the time came for him to die?

Chapter 7

THE MAN WITH THE BELL

Francis Xavier was not the first priest to
come to Goa, a bustling Portuguese outpost
that contained a number of monasteries and
churches. After the Portuguese had established
their colony there, Franciscan and Dominican
monks arrived. But they were busy with parish
duties, and little was done to convert the natives. Someone was needed to act as a spark to

light the fires of mission work, and this spark was to be Francis Xavier.

"I must go to open a way," Francis wrote in one of his letters to Rome. He wanted to get the Church started in all of the colonies. He knew that once he did so, other missioners would come behind him and carry on.

As soon as Francis arrived in Goa, he went to a large hospital to live. He slept on the floor at the hospital so that he would be on hand if anyone needed him. A sick person had only to groan, and Francis was up and at his bedside.

Each day Francis visited the city's prisons. Hundreds of men were crowded together in cells which were dark and foul smelling. He talked to the prisoners, listened to their sorrows, and gave them what comfort he could. They felt that he was the only friend they had.

In the afternoons he went from house to house, begging money for the sick, the poor, and the prisoners. A person had to be really hard hearted to refuse this poorly-clad priest who wanted nothing for himself. Then late in the afternoon he would go about the city and give the money to those who needed it most.

A few days after his arrival in Goa, Francis heard that a large number of lepers were kept locked in a hospital on the outskirts of the city. He hurried to these poor people who were despised and shunned by the rest of mankind. He could never do enough for them, and each Sunday he said Mass for them.

"They have become my very good and devoted friends," Francis wrote in one of his letters.

It was in Goa that he began trying to attract children. He went up and down the street ringing a bell, inviting the people to come to church and study catechism.

"Faithful Christians!" he cried out. "Send your boys and girls and slaves to catechism lessons, for the love of God!"

Francis attracted large crowds in this way. Then he would line the children up and lead them into the church. He made up little poems about the catechism, and he sang them to the children. Then they would all sing the poems together. His teaching became so popular that other priests began using his methods. It was not long before one could hear children and old folks, fishermen and farmers, singing the catechism lessons as they went about their daily tasks.

He was always thinking of others, and never about himself. His shoes became worn through, and his cassock was in tatters. But he never seemed to notice what clothes he had on.

The cassock Francis wore was the only one he had brought from Europe. It had many holes in it. Some Portuguese friends stole it away one night and replaced it with a new one. In the morning Francis put on the new cassock, never noticing that it was not his old one. That night these same friends asked him to supper.

"My, my! You are really doing us honor tonight," said one of the friends when Francis appeared. "You are all dressed up!"

Then for the first time Francis looked at his

cassock, and was surprised to find that he had on a new garment. He was greatly puzzled until his friends told him what they had done.

One night a newcomer arrived in Goa and asked to see Father Francis Xavier about whom he had heard so much.

"There he is over there playing cards," the newcomer was told. He looked and saw Francis sitting with a group of merchants, laughing gaily as he played out his hand.

"Why, he can't be so holy," exclaimed the man. "He's playing cards just like the rest of you."

Just then Francis rose from the card table and excused himself. The newcomer sent his servant to follow the priest and report what mischief he got into next. About a half hour later the servant returned.

"I followed the Father as you told me," said the servant. "He went to a quiet grove of palm trees, knelt down, and began praying. From the wonderful look on his face, he was really talking to God!"

"I can't understand it!" exclaimed the man to his friends. "First he plays cards with men who are far from saintly. Then he goes off and prays."

"You do not know Father Francis," replied one of the man's friends. "He does not play cards for pleasure. He is trying to convert one of the card players to a better life. Father Francis believes that he should be all things to all men."

"If Father Francis ever accepts an invitation to your house for dinner," said another man with a laugh, "you can be sure that he knows about some sin of yours and is trying to get you back in the good graces of God."

"I can't tell you how often he has gone to dinner at the home of some colonist," remarked the man who had first defended Francis, "and ended up by arranging for the master and his wife to be married in the Church."

About this time Francis wrote a long letter to his religious brothers in the Society of Jesus. In it he begs that the Jesuits start a college in

Goa. He also says that more Jesuits are needed as missionaries in Goa. Francis admits that the missionary work is terribly hard, but he adds: "I believe that troubles are a rest for those who delight in the Cross of Christ, and fleeing from troubles is death. What death is so terrible as leaving Christ after having known Him? But what a rest it is to seek not what we want but what Christ wants."

Chapter 8

THE PEARL FISHERS

After Francis had been six months in Goa,
Governor de Sousa sent for the missioner,
whom he had come to respect very much.

"Father Francis," said the governor, "I have
a work of God for you to do. I want you to
work for a while among the Parava people."

The Paravas lived at the very tip of India
near Cape Comorin. They made their living

by fishing for pearls in the warm, blue waters of the Indian Ocean. Some thirty years earlier the Paravas had asked to become Christians. Priests were sent to them and in two years baptized about twenty thousand. However these people had not been taught the catechism since the priests could not speak their language. And after two years the priests returned to their regular work many miles away. Since that time the Parava people had been alone.

Francis knew the story of their conversion. Realizing that these people needed to be taught about Christianity, and that their children had to be baptized, he told the governor he would be happy to go. So one day in late September he boarded a boat and sailed south along the coast to Cape Comorin. He took with him as guides and interpreters three young Paravas who were studying to become priests.

Francis found the Paravas living in an empty, burning country. The homes of these people were miserable, palm-thatched huts. The Paravas were dark-skinned people who wore only a few bits of clothing. They risked their lives diving into the sea, armed only with a knife, to gather up the pearl-bearing oysters. The sea in which they dived was crowded with sharks, and many a diver lost his life to these terrible fish. There were about thirty thousand Paravas, living in thirty villages scattered throughout the sandy, desert land.

"No Portuguese live among the villagers," Francis wrote to Ignatius, "because the country is so terribly barren and poor. The natives know nothing of their religion other than that they are Christians. As soon as I landed, I went from village to village, baptising the children. The children came to me in such crowds that I had no time to say my prayers or to eat or sleep. They cried out to be taught some prayers, and I then began to understand that in very truth of such is the Kingdom of Heaven."

Francis took little rest and ate whatever food was given him. One day going through a pagan village he heard that a woman there was dying and that she was shortly to have a baby.

At once Francis hurried to the house of the sick woman and began telling her of Christ and reading parts of the gospels to her.

The woman asked to be baptized. Francis baptized her, her husband, and her sons and daughters. The woman became well again, and her baby was born. All the people when they heard the news came hurrying to Francis whom they believed had cured her. As a result, everyone in the village, from the headman down, was converted.

After this had happened, Francis went on to the city of Tuticorin. Here he enlisted the aid of those who knew both Portuguese and the Tamil languages. The latter language was the one used by the natives in the part of India where he was working. With the aid of these men, Francis translated all the main prayers and the ten commandments into the Tamil language. Then he memorized them so that he would not need any interpreters to teach the people.

After this Francis went through the city twice a day ringing his bell to gather a crowd.

Then he would teach them, telling those who learned from him to go home and teach their mothers, fathers, brothers and sisters. Every Sunday he gathered all the people and examined them. At the end of the month, when the people knew the prayers, the commandments, the Apostles' Creed, and the Act of Contrition, he baptized them. For four months, Francis did this work in Tuticorin, and when he left he had baptized thousands of Christians.

Francis was very popular with the people and he was always surrounded by large crowds who wanted him to come to their huts and pray for their sick. It was impossible for Francis to do this.

"It would have taken all my time," he said. "I had the children to teach, baptisms to administer, prayers to memorize in the Tamil language, and the dead to bury."

He did not wish to refuse the people entirely, so he sent the children whom he had taught to the homes of the sick. He told them to gather family and neighbors and recite the prayers they had learned. In this way he satisfied the people, and at the same time taught them prayers.

Back and forth between the Parava villages went the missioner from Navarre. In the summer the heat was like fire, and there was no escape from the burning sun. In the wet season when the rains poured down, the paths became a sea of mud. The land was full of wild animals —jackals, tigers, leopards, elephants, vampire bats, crocodiles, and poisonous snakes. But Francis did not worry about wild animals. He prayed alone at night beneath the palm trees, certain that God would protect him.

"Only when he was exhausted," says a man who traveled with him, "would he take two or three hours sleep. After the people had retired for the night, he spent long hours in prayer, under the stars."

One day when Francis was on his way to a Christian village, he passed a pagan temple where lived two hundred Brahman priests. The Brahman priests, having heard about Francis came hurrying from the temple to see him. Francis had no use for them, because they deceived the people and frightened money out of them.

"What do the gods and idols you adore command you to do in order to be saved?" Francis asked of the priests.

"The gods have two commandments for all those wishing to reach heaven," replied an old priest.

"And what are they?" Francis asked.

"The first is not to kill cows but to adore the gods in them," answered the old man. "The second is that the people give money to us."

Francis, who was sitting down, jumped to his feet. He shouted at the top of his voice, so that all could hear, the Ten Commandments and the Creed. Then he delivered a short sermon on Heaven and Hell.

When he was finished the bearded Brahmans agreed that he spoke with great wisdom and that his God was the true God, because all the things he said were very reasonable.

"Then you must be baptized and become Christians," Francis told his hearers.

"Oh, we cannot do that," replied the Brahmans. "What would people think of us if we changed our ways? Then, too, how would we live if we lost the money given to us?"

Francis turned away, saddened in heart at the stubbornness of these men who saw the truth but would not live by it. He longed to have more helpers with him in this vast land where he was the only white man among so many thousands of natives. With this in mind he wrote a letter to Ignatius that was widely printed and read all over Europe.

"Thousands out here fail to become Christians only because there is no one here to teach them," he wrote. "I have often wanted to rush back to the universities of Europe and cry aloud like a madman to those who have more learning than good will. If only the students would use their learning for a good purpose! I could tell them of thousands of souls who miss Heaven and fall into Hell through their neglect.

"Out here, people flock into Church in such numbers that my arms are often numb from baptizing, and my voice gives out completely through endlessly repeating in their language the Creed, the Commandments, the prayers, and a sermon on Heaven and Hell."

Because of his desire for more help in his work among the Paravas, Francis returned to Goa to see if he could find some assistants. He found that two Jesuits had arrived in Goa since his departure. One of them, Francis Mansilhas, returned to the Paravas with him. Also two secular priests and a Portuguese layman came along to help.

Not long after Francis returned to his beloved Paravas, the Badagas, a fierce and warlike tribe, attacked the Paravas and began killing them for having become Christians.

In an attempt to save themselves, the Christians had taken refuge on some rocks out in the sea where they were dying of hunger and thirst.

Without thinking about his own safety. Francis made plans to rescue these poor Christians. He got together twenty small boats, filled them with supplies, and set out to reach the rocks. But it was the monsoon season. The wind was blowing heavy from the south, and the sea was swollen with great waves which flooded the open boats.

For eight days Francis tried to get to the rocks, but it was impossible because of the wind and waves. He had his Parava helpers try to row out to the rocks. When this failed he told the helpers to try towing the boats along from the shore. Finally, everyone was exhausted from the struggle, and he had to give up and wait for better weather.

On shore he set up relief stations to care for the Paravas who had fled from the Badagas. Since the attackers did not have boats, Francis decided that the safest thing for his Christians to do was to remain on the rocks where the Badagas could not reach them.

When the weather was good he traveled between the mainland and the rocks, taking food, water, and clothing to the Christian Paravas. He also traveled up and down the coast visiting villages and begging for food for them.

"I have been along the land route to the Cape," Francis wrote to Father Mansilhas, "to meet the stricken Christians. They made the saddest sight you can imagine, here a group perishing for lack of food, there some old men vainly trying to keep up with the others. And the dead were all about, and husbands in mourning, and wives bringing babies into the world by the roadside, and many other sights to move one to tears. If you had seen what I have seen, you would have been as much heartbroken."

"He was a fearless man," Father Mansilhas said of Francis. "He not only confronted the Bagadas, but also denounced them to their faces."

At last the trouble died down, because Francis brought the matter to the attention of Governor de Sousa. Although the Bagadas were not punished as they should have been, they were at least forced to end their open warfare on the Christians.

As a result of Francis' letters to Europe, more and more priests were being sent as missioners to India. When Francis saw that help was coming, he began to think about the people beyond India—millions of whom had never heard of Christ.

This thought troubled his soul greatly. In his sleep he saw men in distant lands stretching forth their arms as if begging him to come to them. He felt that if he went among these people and made known their needs, help would come there just as it was coming to India. His desire to do this became stronger and stronger. At last he could stand it no longer. He would leave India and go to these people who seemed to have been forgotten.

Chapter 9

A NEW FIELD

Near the end of the summer of 1545, Francis Xavier boarded a small boat to journey to the land now known as Malaya, a long, narrow peninsula jutting down from Siam. It was the time of the summer monsoon and the trip was a dangerous one. There was peril from attack by the fierce pirates who sailed in that part of the Indian Ocean, and there was the risk of wild storms that might sink the boat.

"I met with many dangers on that voyage," Francis wrote to his friends in Rome. "Our ship ran before a wild wind for more than three miles, and during the whole time the rudder was scraping the ocean floor. Had we struck a rock we would have gone to pieces. And had the water become more shallow, we would have been stranded.

"The people on the boat thought that they were doomed to perish in the angry sea. There was great weeping aboard the ship. God used our peril to teach all of us the lesson that we are powerless without His aid, and it was only by His mercy that we were saved. I hope that those aboard will remember the lesson when ashore."

The pilot of this ship led a very bad life, breaking all the commandments and doing many wicked things. Francis made it a point to talk to the man whenever possible. He was very careful to say nothing that would offend the sailor. Francis was so gentle and kind to this hardened sinner that little by little the man became friendly. Finally the sailor told Francis that he had committed many sins, and that as soon as he reached land he would make a good confession.

It was a month before the boat finally arrived at Malacca, a city very much like Goa. As soon as the pilot was safe ashore, he forgot his promise and began leading a bad life again. He avoided meeting Francis and seemed lost in his sins.

Malacca was an important trading center. It had a large, beautiful harbor, crowded with ships from many parts of the world. Many of Malacca's people called themselves Christians, but few led Christian lives or knew much about their religion.

Francis found a hospital to live in and then began translating prayers into the local language. Once again he went along the streets ringing his bell and gathering crowds. Every day he taught the children their catechism.

Once again he was asked to hear confessions for long hours and to tend the sick. At night he went through the city ringing his bell and calling on the people to pray for the souls in Purgatory. The people of Malacca called him "the holy man."

One day Francis was walking along the sea-shore, saying his prayers, when the sinful pilot of the boat that brought him to Malacca came along. The pilot didn't notice Francis until he was almost upon him. When he did see the priest, it was too late to escape.

"Well, Father, when will you hear my confession?" he said in jest, and for want of something better to say.

"When will I hear you?" asked Francis seriously. "Right now in this very place, if you will, as we walk along the shore."

Francis then made the Sign of the Cross to begin the confession. The pilot was trapped, and his words stumbled out. He had not meant to make a complete confession, but as he talked something happened to him, and he began to feel shame for his sins. Before he knew it, he was confessing with great devotion.

Francis took him to a little chapel which was near the beach, and there the man fell to his knees, beat his breast, and sobbed over his sinfulness. From that time on, the pilot went regularly to confession and Communion. Until he died, years later, he led a very holy life. Such was the power of Francis Xavier to touch the souls of men.

Francis did not win people by scolding them. He was interested in their games and amusements. Sometimes when he would come along and find a group playing cards, the men would stop at his approach.

"You are soldiers," he would tell them. "There is no reason for you to live like monks. Go on with your game. Be merry without offending God."

Often he would be invited to the home of one of the merchants for dinner. He was always the life of the party. When he was leaving he would ask to see the cook and he would tell her that he enjoyed her fine dinner and that if she always cooked that well she would become a saint. Thus hosts and servants came to love him.

In January of 1546 Francis left Malacca for the Spice Islands near New Guinea. He sailed through the Java Sea, arriving at Amboina. Here he continued his missionary work, caring for the inhabitants and the many sailors who visited there. While at Amboina, Francis heard about an island called Morotai, in the Pacific Ocean not far from the Philippines, and he became very interested in it.

"In this island many years ago a great many people became Christians," he wrote, "but by the deaths of the priests who baptized them they have been left without teaching. The island of Morotai is very dangerous, because its people often put poison in the food and drink of visitors."

Francis then told members of his society in Rome that he felt he had to go there. It didn't make any difference if he lost his life in doing so; he wished only to serve God. Many of his friends gave him antidotes against poison. He thanked them but would not take the antidotes. He asked only that they remember him in their prayers, which he said were the surest antidote against poison that can be found.

Francis went on to tell more details of the island people as he had learned them from sailors and merchants who had visited the area. This is what he wrote:

"The people are barbarous and full of treachery. They are brownish-yellow in skin rather than black, and are very disagreeable. There are islands where men eat one another. When one of them dies from sickness, his hands and heels are eaten at a great feast. The people are such barbarians that in some islands a man who wishes to have a feast will ask his neighbor for the loan of his father, if he is very old, for eating. In return the host would promise to give his own father when he is old and the neighbor has a feast."

The letter then tells of the great earthquakes

and seaquakes which often rocked the area. He speaks also of mountains which cast forth fire and rock with a great roaring.

Francis sailed for the fearsome island of Morotai in a frail little boat. When he was at sea only a few hours, strong winds arose and began tossing the boat around. Francis took from around his neck a small crucifix he wore. He dipped the crucifix into the sea, asking God to still the waves. Suddenly a wave smashed the crucific from his hand, and it disappeared in the sea.

The next day when the boat landed on a friendly island near-by, he was still sad over his loss. He was walking along the shore towards a village, accompanied by a helper, Fausto Rodriguez. Just then both men saw a crab come walking out of the sea. In one claw the crab carried the missing crucifix, and the priest and his friend stopped in amazement. The crab crawled up to Francis, and the missioner took the crucifix from its claw. Then the crab returned to the sea and disappeared. Francis and Fausto fell to their knees in prayer.

Chapter 10

THE DANGEROUS ISLANDS

Francis sailed for the Spice Islands in May, 1546. He traveled in one of the frail native boats that moved by sail. He was heading for Tenate, where the Portuguese had a fort. The whole island was a volcano which belched smoke and flame, and which Francis used in his sermons as an example of what Hell was like.

Once at Tenate, Francis quietly began his

work of reforming the people. As elsewhere he used the children, gathering them each day, and having them repeat the catechism to their parents and friends. Once again too, Francis lived in a poor, little hospital and cared for the sick.

The first time Francis was preaching on Tenate, he suddenly paused in his sermon. "Let us now offer an Our Father," he said, "for the soul of John Galvano who has just been drowned."

The people were surprised and wondered how Francis could know John Galvano had died when he was at sea. Three days later the wreckage of John Galvano's boat washed up on the beach at Tenate.

Another day, Francis was saying Mass when he turned around and said, "John Arajuo has died this moment on the island of Amboina. This Mass will be said for the repose of his soul. Please remember him in your prayers."

Two weeks later a boat arrived from Amboina and people aboard said that John Arajuo had died at the exact time Francis had made his announcement.

During the late summer when the people of Tenate were busy gathering cloves and other spices, Francis made several trips far into the island where the most savage people lived. He had to go through thick jungles and suffer the attacks of swarms of insects.

The almost-naked natives fled at the approach of the strange white man, but Francis entered their villages and sang hymns. Gradually the people came out of the jungle. Francis then drew them to him with his friendly smile, and patted the heads of children. Soon he and the villagers were friends.

Francis also visited the surrounding islands. He baptized babies, took care of the sick, and did everything he could to make the people love God. Because of the simplicity of the people, Francis found great comfort and happiness in his work. When he had done as much as he could do, he returned to Tenate.

He intended to get a boat and go from there

back to India. But the people on Tenate did not wish to lose their "holy man." They begged him to remain with them. He stayed for three more months. Then he decided to slip away at midnight, while the people were asleep, to avoid all the weeping that would occur if the islanders knew he was leaving.

However, word of his departure leaked out. The people stumbled through the dark, dusty, narrow streets of the town. Francis was unable to hide from them. Tears flowed freely, and Francis felt very unworthy to be so greatly loved by these people. He told the islanders to keep on studying their catechism and to pray every day.

And they did. Thus five years after his visit there, Christianity was still strong on the islands. The people bravely bore persecution and martyrdom from the Mohammedans. Other priests came to reap the harvest Francis had sown.

Francis then sailed down to Amboina. He spent two weeks there hearing confessions, visiting all the Christian villages, and telling the people to be strong in their Faith. His work there was very successful too, because not long afterwards many of these Christians were also put to death by the Mohammedans.

When the Mohammedans tried to make one of Francis' helpers change his religion, he told them: "I know one thing which Father Francis taught me, that it is good to die for Jesus Christ. Because Father said this I cannot become a Mohammedan."

Six hundred of Francis' converts were tortured to death or burned alive. One of them said: "I love my Faith better than life. I am a Christian. If you Moors let me go, I will live as a Christian. If you kill me, I will die as a Christian." This is the brave Christianity Francis left behind him.

Francis sailed from Amboina to Malacca. There he met a Portuguese sea captain and a small man who looked like a Chinese. The captain introduced the small man as Anjiro, a native of the islands of Japan.

"I have heard the seafaring men speak of the islands of Japan," Francis said to Anjiro. "But you are the first native of those islands that I have met. What brings you to Malacca?"

"In Japan," said Anjiro, who spoke Portuguese very well, "I killed a man in a brawl. In order to escape punishment, I took refuge aboard a Portuguese ship that was in the harbor near my home."

"To take the life of another is a power that belongs only to God," declared Francis.

"That I now know," replied Anjiro humbly. "From the good captain here I learned about Christianity. Now I truly repent my crime. I wish to become a Christian, Father, and live according to the law of God. It is for this reason that I have come to you."

"I am about to leave for Goa," Francis told the Japanese. "Come with me. I will tell you about God, and in return you can tell me about Japan, for truly I am very interested in that land."

"I have already promised my friend, the captain, that I will go to Goa with him," answered the Japanese. "I will meet you there."

"So be it!" said Francis.

The news about Japan excited Francis. He could imagine thousands of Japanese like Anjiro begging to become Christians. He wrote a letter to Ignatius Loyola telling him about Japan.

"Some very large islands were discovered a short time ago, called the islands of Japan," Francis wrote. "The people have a great desire to be taught about God."

Francis then went on to tell about Anjiro and the things he said. Anjiro had made a very good impression on him. When he asked Anjiro if the Japanese would become Christians, Anjiro had told him that if the Japanese saw that a man lived what he taught, they would become Christians. They are very reasonable people who do what is right and good.

"I have a strong feeling in my soul," ended the letter, "that before two years are up, I shall go to Japan. Meanwhile we shall teach Anjiro about Christianity and then have him translate our prayers into the Japanese language."

As soon as Francis reached Goa, he started making plans to visit Japan. On the Feast of St. John the Baptist in 1594, all was ready. Francis, Anjiro and a few other men boarded a Chinese junk and set off to convert Japan.

Chapter 11

FRANCIS GOES TO JAPAN

The three-thousand-mile journey to Japan
started off well. The captain of the junk set his
sails to speed along as rapidly as possible. The
junk was a large, lumbering boat but the captain urged every bit of speed he could. He
swung through the straits of Singapore and
then into the South China Sea.

[119]

The ship's captain had a large pagan idol set up on the deck of the junk. Before this he burned incense and sacrificed chickens. He had a pile of sticks which he would shake up and throw out, and then read the future from them. Whenever any decision had to be made, the captain would consult his idol and throw his sticks. Francis was very sad about this pagan worship.

Once in the South China Sea, the captain slowed down his junk. He made frequent stops at the various islands and seemed in no hurry to get to Japan. Francis became uneasy. He feared that something was going wrong. The monsoon winds would not last too long, and if the junk didn't make all the speed possible the travelers might be forced to spend the winter in a Chinese harbor.

Francis learned that one day when the Chinese captain was reading the future from his sticks, he had seen that the junk would reach Japan safely but would not return to Malacca. As a result, he wanted to take the ship to a Chinese port and stay there for the winter, sailing for Japan in the spring. Francis had all he could do to persuade the man to go on with the journey.

Then without warning tragedy struck. The sea became very rough, with great waves. Fearing that the boat would turn over or be driven on rocks, the captain threw out his anchor. Strong winds arose, and before long the junk was swallowed up in a raging typhoon— a terrible storm which comes towards the change of the monsoon season. The junk was battered by wind, rain and waves, and it began to take on water.

A sudden lurch threw Emmanuel, a Chinese convert who was traveling with Francis, into the hold which was partly filled with water. Francis and his helpers went to the boy's aid. While the ship twisted and tossed they climbed into the hold and dragged Emmanuel from the water and up to the deck. The boy was unconscious. He had struck his head and received a deep cut, and he had swallowed a large amount of water. It seemed as if he had drowned.

Francis and the others worked over the

young Chinese. After some time Emmanuel began breathing normally, and then opened his eyes. Although Emmanuel was to be in pain for many days from the wound in his head, Francis was thankful that no more harm had come to him.

Just then a cry went up that the captain's young daughter had been washed overboard by a wave. Everyone rushed to the aid of the girl. The pagan captain who had seen the child vanish before his eyes was moaning with wild grief. The girl had already disappeared beneath the angry sea, and nothing could be done for her.

Francis was full of sorrow at her loss, and he was further saddened to see the way the captain and his crew carried on. The Chinese wailed and moaned. They burned incense before the idol, and offered food and drink. They also killed chickens as sacrifices. For a day and night the Chinese crew prayed before the idol, all the while the wind roared and great seas washed the decks.

Finally the captain cast lots to learn why his daughter had died. When the sticks were read, they said that if Emmanuel had been allowed to perish, as the gods wanted, the girl would not have drowned. The gods wanted a human sacrifice, and when they could not have Emmanuel they took the young girl.

Francis got little sleep that night. The Chinese crew was muttering and threatening. It seemed as if at any moment he and his helpers might be thrown overboard. Francis prayed that God would not allow the devil to triumph, for he was sure that the devil was working through the lots.

"You can see how our lives hung on those lots of the devil," he wrote later to Ignatius, "for we were in the power of his servants. What would have become of us if God had allowed the devil to work all the mischief he desired?"

The next morning dawned clear. The storm had vanished, and the sea had gone down. The captain ordered the anchor of the junk raised, and the journey was started again. But the captain had no intention of going to Japan. If he had followed his own mind in the first place, he would have gone directly to China. Then the junk might have missed the storm, and his daughter might still be alive. Francis begged and pleaded, but the man would not change his mind.

At last the junk reached the harbor of Canton. The captain said that the travelers could spend the winter aboard the boat in the harbor. Francis begged him to steer on for Japan. There seemed, however, to be no way to make the captain change his mind. At last, unwillingly, Francis decided that they would have to stay in Canton. Then for no apparent reason, the captain announced that he was taking the ship to another harbor, the port of Chang-Chow. He ordered the anchor up and directed the junk out to the China Sea again.

Chang-Chow was further north and therefore nearer Japan, but it was far from satisfactory to Francis. He wanted to reach Japan, and he prayed that God would find some way to get him and his helpers there. His prayer was answered in a strange way.

The junk was just about to enter the harbor of Chang-Chow, when another junk came sailing out. The captains greeted each other, and the departing captain warned Francis' boat not to go into the harbor.

"The place is full of pirates," he shouted across the water. "If you enter, you are lost."

The pagan captain didn't know what to do. If he went into the harbor, the pirates would take his boat and perhaps his life. Yet he could not return to Canton since the last of the monsoon was blowing from the south, and there was no way of going against it. There was nothing to do but head for Japan, two weeks away.

Francis looked forward to the end of the voyage with great eagerness. All during the trip Anjiro, who had been baptized and given the name of Paul, had been teaching Japanese to Francis and the other members of the party.

He was also instructing them in the ways of Japanese life. Now that learning could be put to use.

Young Brother Juan Fernandez, who had been a wealthy dandy before meeting Francis, learned rapidly. Francis and Father Cosmas de Torres, a Spanish priest Francis had met in Amboina and received into the Jesuits, found difficulty in remembering Japanese.

"What port are you making, captain?" Francis asked the Chinese.

"With the way the wind is blowing," he replied, "there is only one port we can make. Kagoshima."

Here was an unexpected piece of good fortune! Kagoshima was Anjiro's hometown. It would be a fine place to start the work of converting Japan. Anjiro's relatives and friends would be of great help.

Francis was full of joy. He even felt kindly towards the captain who had caused so much delay. He considered him a good fellow, and forgave his stubborness, saying that he was a pagan and did not know any better. Later in Kagoshima the captain was to take sick and die. Francis was to write to the governor of Malacca about him.

"All through the voyage," said the letter, "he was good to us. But he died without believing in the True God."

Francis felt that he was guilty of a great failure because he had not converted the captain. But he blamed himself without cause, because he had done everything possible.

However, as the junk sailed through the narrow opening to the land-locked harbor at Kagoshima, no thought of the captain's death was in Francis' mind. He stood at the rail of the boat, looking at the green hills of Japan.

Ahead he could see the tiled and thatched roofs of the city of Kagoshima. On an island at the head of the bay stood the great volcano Sakurajima, smoke rising from its cone.

On the green hillsides around the bay, Francis could see neatly terraced fields in which rice was grown. Above the fields were rows of trees—cherry and orange orchards. Here and there in the fields and among the trees he could make out small figures busily at work. Everything showed that the people took good care of their fields, crops, and homes.

As the junk pulled into the docks at Kagoshima, Francis saw men and women hurrying down to the ship. The women were small and were dressed in beautiful kimonos. The men were sturdy, some dressed in kimonos, others wearing clothing for work in the fields.

At Francis' side stood Anjiro, rapidly pointing out the sights of his homeland which he had not seen for so many years. Anjiro chattered on excitedly, but Francis heard little that he said. The missioner's heart was singing. To him Japan appeared as the Promised Land.

To himself he said, "What a world is this to win for Christ!"

Chapter 12

THE LAND OF THE RISING SUN

At the time Francis Xavier arrived in Japan,
the government of that country was very mixed
up. Francis thought of Japan as a place where
the emperor ruled the country and was assisted
by governors of provinces, as was done in
Europe. Francis had drawn up his plans for
winning Japan on this belief.

Actually, conditions were quite different from what Francis had imagined. Although Japan had an emperor, he had no real power. He was looked upon by the people as a religious chief. Before Japan was discovered by the Europeans, the real ruler of the country was the *shogun,* the man who controlled the army. But at the time Francis arrived, even this man had little power.

The local governors, or *daimyos,* did as they pleased. They made laws and collected taxes. They were like kings of small kingdoms. They held great power in their own areas, and each had his own army of knights, or *samurai.*

The greatest power was held by the *bonzes,* or Buddhist monks. They too did as they pleased and took orders from no one. They were rich and lived well. Many of the monasteries had their own armies. To become a monk, a man had to be able to handle weapons with great skill. The monks caused many civil wars and were feared by emperor, shogun and daimyo alike.

When Francis and his friends went ashore at Kagoshima, they received a warm welcome. Anjiro took them to his own house to live. While he had been away, his family had made a settlement with the family of the man he had killed, and the charges against him had been dropped. People crowded into the house every day to see both Anjiro and the strange white men he had brought home with him.

Francis was struck by the politeness of the people. He found the Japanese to be men and women of honor. He was surprised to discover that all of the men from the age of fourteen carried daggers and swords. Almost all of the people were able to read and write. He found that they hated lies, that they wanted to hear about God, and that they did not gamble.

Some of the Japanese customs were difficult for Francis to follow and hard for him to understand. The Japanese were always bowing, and at first Francis thought that they overdid this, but gradually he came to think of it as a form of politeness. He found it difficult to sit on the floor most of the day. The Japanese did not have chairs in their homes. They squatted on the floor, sitting on their heels.

Another difficult custom was eating with chopsticks. The Japanese did not use knives and forks. Instead they used two thin bamboo sticks. With these pieces of wood, they picked up food from their plates. It was very hard to get used to eating with these sticks.

Francis also learned that many Japanese customs were the opposite of the customs of Europe. Just as a European would take off his hat and stand up to greet a visitor, a Japanese would take off his shoes and sit down. When a Japanese went into mourning he put on white clothes instead of the black clothes that a European would wear. When a Japanese wanted to celebrate, he would dress in black or purple, the colors of sadness in Europe. When writing a letter, a Japanese would begin at the bottom of the page in the right hand corner, just opposite the way a European would write a letter.

"They are the best race yet discovered,"

Francis wrote, despite the many differences. "And I think that among non-Christians their match will not easily be found."

Not long after the arrival of the strangers, the excitement that their coming caused reached the Castle of Kokubu, some fifteen miles from Kagoshima. Here lived the rich and powerful daimyo of Satsuma. When he heard of the strangers, he sent for Anjiro and questioned him carefully about the things he had seen outside Japan and about the men who had arrived with him in Kagoshima. He was very polite and said that he would be happy to meet Francis.

Francis called at the castle and was received kindly. The daimyo told him that he was free to preach the Christian religion and make converts. At that time, Francis did not know what was in the back of the mind of the Japanese governor. The man realized that if the Portuguese would start trading with Japan through the port of Kagoshima, great wealth would come to his land. If he was kind to Francis, he thought the missioner might persuade the Portuguese to open trade.

Back in Kagoshima, Francis and his friends spent the winter translating prayers and studying the Japanese language. Francis found it an almost impossible language to learn, as did Father Torres. But young Brother Fernandez made much progress. During all of his time in Japan, Francis had to depend upon interpreters to get his message over to the Japanese people. He found the language so difficult that it took him forty days to memorize the Japanese translation of the ten commandments.

Of course, Francis did more than merely study language. He preached to the people through interpreters. He taught hundreds the catechism of the Christian faith. He visited Buddhist monasteries and tried to convert the bonzes. Anjiro was also busy preaching, and he converted many, many people.

When Francis went to a monastery, he would sit down on the steps, take out a book in which he had written the Japanese for the sermon he had prepared, and start to read. Soon a crowd would gather around. Even though his Japanese had a terrible accent, the people listened politely, and some remained to ask him further questions.

It was from such a crowd that Francis converted a young Japanese, whom he later baptized as Bernard. This young man was to travel with Francis and act as his interpreter. Later, Francis sent him to Portugal, where he became a member of the Society of Jesus and impressed everyone with his wisdom and holiness. Bernard told the other Jesuits how much he owed Francis Xavier.

"For seven months," he said, "I slept in the same room with him. He took only very little sleep during which I heard him sigh and invoke the name of Jesus. With my own eyes I have seen Father Francis cure many sick people of their illnesses. We would make the Sign of the Cross over them, sprinkle them with holy water, and they would be instantly cured."

Another Japanese who was converted by Francis was the manager of a castle where lived a well-to-do samurai. Francis named this man Michael. After Michael was baptized he hurried back to the castle and told everyone of the great prize that had been given him. He taught all those who lived at the castle, and then sent for Francis to come and baptize the people who were ready. Francis baptized fifteen there, among them the wife of the samurai and his daughter. Michael promised that he would make more converts and care for those already made.

Although some six hundred converts had been made in Kagoshima, conversions were not being made as rapidly as Francis wished. Then too the daimyo had turned against him, since he had brought no Portuguese traders to Kagoshima. Therefore, the daimyo let it be known that he no longer cared for his people to become Christians.

"Almost all of the people would have become Christians," Francis wrote to his superiors, "but the bonzes kept them from it."

Francis goes on to relate how the bonzes

told the daimyo that the law of God which Francis taught was different from his law. These Buddhist monks made the daimyo believe that the Christians might not obey him. He then sent out word that anyone who became a Christian would be put to death, although those who were already Christians might keep their religion.

After this announcement Francis knew that any more work in Kagoshima would be hopeless. So he decided to move on. First he would go to Hirado, another port where a Portuguese boat had just arrived. Then he would go to Kyoto where the emperor lived. He thought that if he could get the permission of the emperor to preach Christianity, no daimyo would be able to stop him.

He went to Hirado, visited the Portuguese ship there, and arranged for several of his best converts to be taken to Goa for education. He also wrote letters to be sent back to Goa and Portugal. Then he returned to Kagoshima for the last time. He told the Christians that he was leaving, and there was much weeping and sadness.

Anjiro, who had given Francis the idea of journeying to Japan, was left behind to care for the Christians at Kagoshima, while Francis and his assistants went on to Hirado. Francis did not remain here long, but he did make a few converts even in the short time.

Leaving Father Torres to care for the Christians at Hirado, Francis, Brother Fernandez, and Bernard, the Japanese convert, took a boat to Hakata. They had to pass through seas where pirates pounced on passing ships.

They hid in the hold of their boat so that pirates would not find them. On land things were much worse and they had to go overland on their way to Honshu. Winter had come, and the travelers had to make their way through snow storms and freezing weather.

At night they would take shelter in a poor inn, and many times they were refused shelter by innkeepers. Once going over a mountain they were caught in a terrible snow storm. Almost frozen with the cold, their legs became swollen and they could hardly walk. Icy winds blew down upon them, and they dared not rest for fear they would freeze and die. Completely worn out, their clothes in tatters, and half starved, the missioners finally arrived in Yamaguchi, the second largest city in Japan.

Francis and his friends looked so much like beggars that they had a hard time finding a place to live. A man named Uchida finally took them into his home, and for this kindness God blessed him. Uchida and his wife were the first two converts in Yamaguchi.

The main goal Kyoto was still many miles away, but while recovering from their hard journey, Francis decided that they should preach in the streets. Twice a day they went out and gathered crowds. The people poked fun at them, and the children mocked them. Only a few showed interest in what the missioners preached.

At times the crowds became angry and threatening. At any moment Brother Fernandez expected to see the Japanese draw their swords and kill the missioners. He told Francis his worry.

"There is nothing that needs more control than the fear of death," Francis replied. "Despise death and these men will respect you, and know our teaching is from God."

For many days the missioners kept on preaching. Brother Fernandez and Bernard did most of the talking, while Francis stood aside praying. However, the people of Yamaguchi had hard hearts. Few cared to hear the word of God.

One day Francis and Brother Fernandez were ordered to appear before the powerful Yamaguchi daimyo. When they arrived at the palace they were led into a large room where the daimyo received important persons. Francis and Brother Fernandez made two deep bows, as was the custom. In chambers off this room, the samurai and nobles were gathered.

The daimyo asked many questions about India and Europe, and then said he would like to hear about the religion that the missioners had come to Japan to teach. Brother Fernandez read from his notebook the sermon Francis had written on the ten commandments. Then he read another sermon which denounced certain sins of which the daimyo was guilty.

"When I read this passage the daimyo became thoroughly upset by it, and anger showed in his face," Brother Fernandez said later. "I was afraid that he might order our heads off then and there."

The Yamaguchi daimyo, while amazed at their rashness, merely ordered them to leave. He would not give Francis permission to go on preaching and baptizing.

"With all this," Francis wrote, "very few became Christians. Seeing the small amount of fruit gained, we made up our minds to go on to Kyoto, the main city of all Japan."

Chapter 13

THE GREAT DISAPPOINTMENT

There is in the city of Kyoto today a painting which shows Francis Xavier arriving in
the capital of Japan. It pictures him running
barefoot in the snow behind the sedan chair of
a nobleman. Behind him in the snow he has
left footprints colored red with his blood. His
clothes are tattered and he appears starving,
but on his face is a look of peace and great joy.

[143]

The painting sums up what Francis went through to reach Kyoto, and the great hopes he brought there with him.

The first part of the journey from Yamaguchi to Kyoto had to be made over rough roads. Francis and his friends covered forty miles to reach the port of Iwakuni. Snow drifts came up to their knees. They had to cross freezing mountain torrents that were waist deep. The region was full of unfriendly samurai who at any moment might wish to test their swords on the missioners.

Children chased them, throwing stones. Their clothes became so tattered that innkeepers refused them shelter. Often they could obtain no food and had to munch a bit of dry rice which they carried with them. At Sakai, no inn would accept them, and they had to build a crude hut on a mountainside to escape the cold driving rain and snow.

The travelers had to remain some time at Sakai, because a small war was being fought between there and Kyoto. While at Sakai children tormented them, and they were unable to preach. Adults too poked fun at the ragged strangers. One young man called Francis a fool and a stupid beast.

"Why do you speak to me in this way?" Francis asked. "I love you very much and I would greatly like to teach you the way of salvation."

But the young man laughed at Francis' kindness, and kept on mocking him.

Finally the travelers were permitted to join a nobleman who was going to the capital. This man allowed them to follow his party as his servants did. He also insisted that Francis, Brother Fernandez, and Bernard carry some of his baggage on their backs. It was a hard journey because the servants who carried the sedan chair in which the nobleman rode moved at a brisk trot. Francis and his friends had to run to keep up with the nobleman. The painting in Kyoto shows the end of this part of the journey.

It was with a happy heart that Francis entered Kyoto. Here was the end of his trail. Here he would see the emperor of all Japan and get permission to preach over the whole country. Then came the great disappointment.

Once in the city, Francis saw that great areas had been burnt out and destroyed in the war then going on. The temples were badly in need of repair. Almost half the houses in the city lay in ruins. Every attempt to see the emperor failed, and after Francis learned that even the Emperor's own people did not obey him, he stopped trying to see the man.

Because of the war, the people were not interested in listening to the teachings of Christ. There were a few attempts at preaching, but they were not successful. Only a handful of converts were made.

Francis remained only eleven days in Kyoto —eleven days of bitter disappointment. Then realizing that because of the war nothing could be done in the city, he decided to return to Yamaguchi. On the face of things, it would appear that Francis Xavier had failed. But he had not. The seed of religion which he had planted in Kyoto in his brief visit there would blossom into a rich harvest. Only a dozen years later, Kyoto would boast many, many Christians. From this city came some of the greatest martyrs the Church has ever produced.

In order not to travel overland and risk the many dangers, the party left Kyoto by boat. The journey in a small open boat in freezing weather was far from pleasant. When they reached Osaka, they took passage on another boat to Sakai. Finally they were back to Hirado, their starting point four or five months earlier.

Their hardships were greatest on the return journey. It was February, the time of snow, sleet, and wind. The missioners had neither rest nor shelter. Francis would buy dry fruits at the inns and carry them in his sleeves. Then when he came across children by the roadside, he would give them some of the fruit and his blessing.

Once safe in Hirado, Francis thought over

the whole unhappy journey he had just finished. He felt that it had been a failure. He had been hooted at and stoned. He had not been well received by daimyos or the emperor. No one had been impressed with the missioners. Perhaps it was because they looked so shabby. Perhaps if they went dressed as ambassadors—ambassadors of God—they would be better received.

Once again Francis' high spirits came back to him. At once he began making plans to return to Yamaguchi and visit the powerful daimyo there. This time he would impress that ruler.

Francis ordered a new kimono for himself and one for Brother Fernandez. He had them made of the best silk. He and Brother Fernandez had once been dandies, dressing in the best style. He would show the daimyo that he knew how to dress! Kimonos were also ordered for Bernard and another Japanese Christian. They were given swords and daggers to wear, as was the custom among the rich people. The Indian boy, Amador, was dressed in the finest silks, which made his dark skin shine even brighter.

Even then Francis was not finished. Opening the many presents he had brought from India and which had rested all this time in the care of Father Torres, he chose the ones he thought would make the best impression. Then he finally wrapped up in silk two letters he had never used—one from the governor of India; the other from the Bishop of Goa.

This time Francis traveled in the style that befit an ambassador. He hired horses for his friends, and for himself a sedan chair. He entered Yamaguchi with great pomp. The daimyo, who heard of his impressive approach, at once invited him to his palace.

Francis greeted the daimyo, never mentioning the reprimand he had had Brother Fernandez deliver on his last visit. He presented his friends to the Japanese ruler. Then he gave the daimyo his gifts. They included a music box, a glass mirror, a three-barreled rifle, yards of the best cloth, books, vases, paintings, barrels of port wine, and a grandfather clock. The daimyo was thrilled by the gifts, particularly by the clock which sounded chimes whenever it reached the hour.

The daimyo wanted to give Francis a large gift of money in return, but the missioner wisely refused the present. He asked only that he and his friends be allowed to preach and baptize. The daimyo agreed at once. He ordered his assistants to prepare a large empty monastery which he turned over to Francis to use as long as he remained in Yamaguchi. He also ordered a notice to be written and put up around the city.

It said: "I am pleased to allow that the Law of God may be taught and preached throughout my lands and that those who wish to convert may do so freely. My servants are all forbidden to hinder any of the Fathers who preach this Law."

Francis' plan had proved a great success. If Japan was not to be won one way, another would do!

At first the work in Yamaguchi went slowly. One day when Brother Fernandez was preaching in the street, surrounded by a large crowd, a rough looking fellow began to make fun of him. When Brother Fernandez did not notice him, the man spat in Brother's face, the worst insult that could be offered to a Spanish gentleman.

Brother Fernandez did not pause in his sermon, nor did he show any anger. He simply wiped the spittle off as he went on talking. A man in the crowd, hostile to the Christians, watched what had happened. When he saw how Brother Fernandez acted, he suddenly realized that here was a man who practiced what he preached. As soon as the sermon ended, he followed Francis and Brother to their monastery and asked to be prepared for baptism. He was the first convert in Yamaguchi.

From that time on converts came in dozens. In the first two months after the incident five hundred people were taught and baptized. All of the missioners were busy every day teaching. Twice a day large crowds came to the monastery to hear Brother Fernandez explain the Law of God, and among the visitors were many Buddhist monks and nuns, some of whom became converts.

On another day when the missioners were preaching in the street, a minstrel, who went from house to house among the rich, entertaining with song and story, was in the crowd. Impressed with what he heard, he approached Francis and said that he wanted to leave behind his stories, songs and violin, and work only to serve God. Francis taught this minstrel, who was blind in one eye and nearly so in the other, and baptized him with the name Lawrence.

Lawrence became the first Brother in Japan of the Society of Jesus. This poor, misshapen man was the greatest convert Francis Xavier ever made. Lawrence debated with the most learned Buddhist monks, and he always defeated them. The power of his teaching was so great that the most learned men in Japan humbled themselves at his feet. He made thousands of converts, and he was the missioner who went to Kyoto and began the movement there towards the Church.

Once when Brother Lawrence was preaching in a Buddhist monastery to three hundred samurai, he badly defeated a monk who tried to debate with him. The man grabbed a sword, and rushed at Brother shouting, "I'll show you how immortal your soul is!" The maddened monk was held back by others. Brother Lawrence faced many such dangers, but he never weakened in his work. He lived a very holy life, and died at an old age in Nagasaki.

The Christian Faith was growing well in Yamaguchi, when one day a letter reached Francis from the daimyo of Bungo, inviting the missioner to come there to preach Christianity. It was a wonderful chance to win more souls. Francis took with him three of his Japanese converts—Bernard, John and Matthew— and left at once for Bungo. Father Torres was placed in charge of the work at Yamaguchi, and Brother Fernandez was left behind to help him.

When Francis reached a port on the seacoast, he found a Portuguese ship riding at anchor. It was a pleasure for him to see and talk with men from Europe. He was soon busy hearing confessions and saying Mass for the Portuguese sailors. The captain of the ship, Duarte de Gama, was an old friend of Francis, and this man offered to take Francis to the city where the daimyo of Bungo lived.

Francis arrived in Bungo in great style. He saw the daimyo and was received kindly. The daimyo told him that he could preach Christianity to the people. Francis was happy at this permission, but he was worried because the Portuguese ship had brought no mail or news of the Jesuits in Europe. Francis had written shortly after arriving in Japan, asking for more helpers, and so far not a single word had come about them.

Francis decided that he must travel back to India and learn what had happened. The presence of the Portuguese boat was heaven-sent, because the boat could take him part way back to India. Once he had settled his business there, he would return to Japan. The whole trip should take less than a year. He sent Father Torres money to carry on the work in Yamaguchi. Then he boarded the Portuguese vessel.

It was November, 1551, when Francis saw the islands of Japan disappear over the horizon behind his ship.

Chapter 14

THE LAST VOYAGE

Somewhere on that journey back to India, Francis Xavier decided to go to China. The thought had been in the back of his mind for a long time. In Japan he had had his prayers translated into Chinese. He had long prayed for the conversion of the whole Orient, and for a time he thought that the way to do it was to convert Japan. Gradually, the idea came that

China was the key. By the time he reached India, his mind was made up—China would be his next goal.

Before going to Goa, he visited the governor of India. He told the governor that he wanted to go to China as soon as possible. His experiences in Japan convinced him that the first visit must be done in grand style. An ambassador should be appointed to go with him. They must be loaded down with presents. The governor agreed and appointed a rich merchant.

Francis then went on to Goa. When the people of Goa saw the tall, lean priest with black flashing eyes and broad smile, descend from the ship, they greeted him as joyously as if he had returned from the dead. He was happy to be back at the scene of his first mission work, but also anxious to start his new work in China.

On the journey home Francis learned that he had been named head of all the Jesuits in the Far East. Therefore, in Goa he had many bits of business to arrange because of his job as superior. The college at Goa was very badly organized, and he had to set things straight. All other odds and ends also had to be put in order. Francis hurried to work, and before long things were running smoothly.

Those Jesuits who had known him earlier were saddened to see how time had changed Francis. He had grown much older. His beard was streaked with white, and his once coal black hair had become grey. His health was also bad. He seemed to be but skin and bones, and he had stomach trouble although he never complained about it.

But the most distressing thing was that he seemed completely worn out. He needed a long rest, but he refused to take it while there was yet work to be done. He insisted on preaching four and five times a day, sitting long hours in the confessional, caring for the sick, and taking care of anyone who called upon him for help. Francis was busy every moment during the two months he spent in Goa.

Meanwhile, Francis was also making arrangements for his departure for China. He found passage on a ship, made the necessary purchases, and wrote many letters to Jesuits in the Orient and Europe. One letter to Ignatius ended with the signature: "Your least and most exiled son, Francis." He did not know it but at that very time Ignatius had decided to recall Francis to Rome to help him direct the Society, which had now grown very large. However, Francis was already dead when the letter arrived in Goa that would have called him back.

Finally the time came for Francis to leave. His boat was to sail on the day before Good Friday. In the morning Francis said the Mass at the college and gave Holy Communion to the students.

But a lack of wind becalmed his ship in the harbor, and it was Easter Sunday before the voyage got underway. Francis and his friends thought it a very favorable day on which to begin their trip. There were many tears when the boat carrying Francis left Goa. A large number of people never expected to see Francis again, because no European was allowed to enter China. Those who tried to do so were either killed or cast into prison. Many thought that this fate would befall Francis if he tried to get into China.

Sailing with Francis on that Easter Sunday were Anthony, a very holy Chinese youth, and Christopher, an Indian. There were also two Brothers and a priest destined for service in Japan. Aboard the ship were many rich presents for the emperor of China.

During the first month of the voyage, the ship met a very terrible storm, and the sailors thought that they would surely perish. Much of the cargo had to be thrown overboard to keep the boat from sinking. Francis cheered the sailors by promising them that God would save the ship.

Francis then went up to the captain's deck. He blessed the sea, begging God to have mercy. He kept on praying until the winds and waves died down. Perhaps the storm was a warning of what lay ahead, because Francis was troubled during the rest of the voyage that the devil would find a way to keep him from reaching China. He mentioned this worry to many of those aboard ship.

When he reached Malacca, he found that he had reason for his fears. The captain of the port was jealous of the trader who had been given the high post of Francis' ambassador. The captain refused to let the trader take his boat from the port. He even put the rudder of the trader's ship under guard so that it would be impossible to sail the ship.

Francis tried to change the mind of the captain, but that man would not budge. When papers were shown from the Bishop of Goa and the governor, ordering Francis to go to China and appointing the trader as his ambassador, the captain grabbed the papers, threw them on the floor, spat on them, and crushed them under his foot.

"That's what I think of the governor and his orders," said the captain. "The priest can go where he will, but the trader will not."

The captain spread all sorts of rumors about Francis and turned many of the people against the missioner. Francis did not dare go abroad in the day because the people insulted him with foul names.

At last wishing to be rid of Francis, the jealous captain told him that he might sail in the trader's ship, although the trader himself would not be permitted to go with him. Francis decided that he would go alone without the ambassador. He also announced that when he had left Europe he had been given certain powers by the Pope, and he was using those powers to excommunicate the wicked captain because he had interfered with the work of conversions. He sent several letters to Goa asking that the excommunication be proclaimed all over India so that future missioners would not have the same trouble he did.

When it came time to leave Malacca, a priest who lived there asked Francis if he forgave the wicked captain.

"I have no bitterness against him," Francis

replied. "But the only place I shall see him again is at the Day of Judgment."

Then Francis knelt down and prayed for the man who had done him so much evil. Arising, he took off his shoes and shook the dust of Malacca from them, as Christ told the Apostles to do when they were rejected.

"Is this parting forever?" asked the Malacca priest.

"That is as God wills," replied Francis, jumping into the small boat which was to take him to the ship in the harbor. As soon as he was aboard, the ship, which was named *Holy Cross,* lifted anchor and moved away. Except for a brief stop at Singapore, the mainland of Asia was never again to see Saint Francis Xavier alive.

Chapter 15

THE END OF THE JOURNEY

The *Holy Cross* could not take Francis directly to China because foreigners were not allowed to enter that country. So the boat did the next best thing. It put in at Sancian Island, a small bit of land about six miles off the China coast. This island was a meeting place for Portuguese ships in the harbor when the *Holy Cross* arrived, as well as a number of Chinese junks.

From some of the Portuguese sailors who had been captured by the Chinese, Francis heard of the terrible underground dungeons in which captives were herded and chained to the ground. The sailors spoke of savage tortures and starvation. But they did not frighten Francis with their tales. He would dare anything for Christ!

The Portuguese sailors wanted nothing to do with Francis' project. They feared for their own safety. They did, however, help him to build a little wooden hut with a straw roof. Here he said Mass, heard confessions, preached, and taught the slaves and children from the ships and the few crude houses around the harbor.

Francis talked to many of the Chinese merchants who came to Sancian to trade. None of them dared smuggle him into China. No matter how much Francis begged them, they refused, saying that if they were caught not only would they lose their fortunes, but even their very lives.

But at last Francis found one merchant willing to take the risk. The Chinese would not accept Francis aboard his own boat, but for two hundred dollars worth of pepper he promised to send a junk which would be manned by his sons and servants.

"This way the secret will be better kept," said the Chinese. "And if something goes wrong, I will not be connected with the smuggling. I will also arrange a place near the city gate where you can hide for three or four days."

"I am very grateful to you," Francis replied.

The merchant then left for China to arrange the business. Francis' Portuguese friends told the missioner that he was foolish to trust the merchant.

"He may have you killed as soon as you are aboard the junk," said one sailor, "and dump your body into the sea. That way he will collect the pepper and still run no risk."

"If you aren't killed," declared a Portuguese merchant, "the Chinese may cast you upon one

[167]

of the many uninhabited islands off the coast. You would then die from thirst or starvation."

"I must trust the man," replied Francis.

"But, Father, even if the man keeps his word," the merchant went on, "the governor of Canton will certainly throw you into prison."

"I know the risk," said Francis. "But the danger of all dangers is to lose trust in God. To distrust God would be a far more terrible thing than any other evil. If God is for us, who can overcome us?"

As the days dragged on, Francis fell ill with fever. Anthony and Christopher had also been sick, but the missoner had nursed them back to health. Now they cared for him as he lay in the crude little beach shack, burning one moment and freezing the next. He kept one of the boys always on watch for the junk from the mainland. One by one the Portuguese ships pulled up anchor and sailed away, until only the *Holy Cross* was left in the harbor. A letter written about this time shows that Francis was thinking of a second plan in case this first one failed.

"We go with God's help, Anthony, Christopher and myself," he wrote. "Pray much to God for us as we run the very gravest risk of being made captives. But we are happy with the thought that it is much better to be a captive for the love of God than to be free by running away from the Cross. In case our man does not come for us, I shall go to Siam and then to Canton in the fleet which Siam sends to that city."

The November days passed one by one. The weather turned cold, and biting winds roared through the poorly built hut in which Francis and his friends lived. Food ran low, and Francis had to send Anthony to the Portuguese ship to beg for some bread. The merchant's junk was long overdue, but Francis clung to the hope that he would still get to China. He sent a message to the Chinese merchant saying that he would give an extra hundred dollars worth of pepper if the man kept his word.

On November 21, Francis said Mass for a Portuguese man who had died on the island. After Mass, Anthony noticed that Francis was very sick. The Chinese youth suggested that it might be a good idea for Francis to go out to the *Holy Cross*. He could rest aboard the ship and get some warm food. Francis promised he would think about it.

The next day Francis asked Anthony to row him out to the ship. He spent the night aboard the *Holy Cross* but the rolling and tossing of the boat made his fever unbearable. Some sailors brought him back to the island the next morning. He was so ill that a Portuguese merchant carried him to his hut.

"You are very sick, Father Francis," said the Portuguese, kindly. "You should be bled. If you wish I will do it for you."

"I am not used to being bled," Francis replied weakly. "But I leave myself in your hands. Do whatever you think is best for me."

The merchant decided to bleed the priest right away. He took out a knife and cut into a vein in the missioner's wrist, in the belief that the fever and disease would also leave the sick man's body with the blood. The merchant was not skillful at bleeding, and his cutting was so painful that Francis fainted. When he came to, he was so sick that he could not even swallow water.

The next day the merchant bled Francis once again, and the missioner fainted as on the previous day. He could hold no food in his stomach, and he seemed to have no strength to get well.

"Jesus, Son of David, have mercy on me!" Francis said many times as Anthony knelt by his bedside and tried to cool the priest's forehead. On the eighth day of his illness, Francis lost his power to speak, and for three days was silent. During that time he ate nothing and recognized no one. Death seemed always at hand, but from somewhere deep inside of him Francis was finding the courage to keep fighting.

About noon on Thursday, December 1,

Francis suddenly regained his senses. He spoke of God and prayed to the Blessed Trinity. He seemed to know that he was dying, but there was no fear in him. If his mind went back to his boyhood in Navarre, or his student days in Paris, he gave no sign of it.

"Jesus, Son of David, have mercy on me!" Francis repeated over and over. Sometimes he added, "O Virgin, Mother of God, remember me!"

The hours dragged along. Anthony did what he could to make Francis comfortable in his last agony. The Chinese youth propped up a crucifix so that Francis could see it at all times. The dying man did not take his eyes off it but kept on praying. The hours of Friday passed, and Saturday began.

Shortly before dawn on Saturday morning, Anthony was alone with Francis. The Chinese youth heard him gasping for breath. He realized that the end was fast approaching. Anthony lit a candle and placed it in Francis' hand. The dying man looked over the candlelight at the crucifix.

"Jesus!" he whispered.

Francis closed his eyes and quietly sank back, as if going to sleep. Anthony blew the candle out. He knew that his friend was dead.

Chapter 16

THE DAYS AFTER

When it was daylight, Anthony rowed out to the *Holy Cross*.

"The holy Father Francis is dead," Anthony told the sailors aboard ship. "He died just before dawn."

"We will go back with you and help you bury him," said some of the sailors.

They went back to shore with Anthony, but they were soon shivering in the damp, cold weather. They helped build a rough, wooden coffin, and as soon as it was finished they hurried back to the ship.

Anthony dressed the missioner's body in the Mass vestments of a priest. Then he and the kind Portuguese merchant placed the body in the coffin. They carried the wooden box to a rowboat and took it to another part of the island. They dug a deep grave and lowered the box into it.

"It would be a good idea to fill the coffin with lime," said the merchant. "We could put some above the body and some below. The lime will eat away all the flesh and leave only the bones. Then if you wish to take the body back to India for burial later, the bones will be easy to recover."

Anthony thought that this was a good idea. He went to the *Holy Cross* and obtained four sacks of lime. The sacks were emptied into the coffin—two sacks below the body, two sacks covering the body. The top of the coffin was nailed closed, and the grave was filled. Anthony then put stones around the grave as markers so that it could be found.

For over two months the body of Francis Xavier rested in its Sancian Island grave. When favorable winds came in the middle of February, the captain of the *Holy Cross* decided that it was time to sail back to Malacca.

"Please, captain," begged Anthony, "do not sail without the body of Father Francis. He has done so much for others. He should be given Christian burial."

"It is out of the question!" said the captain angrily. "The body will be decaying. It will be foul smelling. It could be a source of disease to the people aboard ship."

"But we covered it with lime," said Anthony. "By this time the lime has eaten away all the flesh. There can be nothing but bones left."

"Well, I will send a couple of men to look," said the captain at last. "If it is not in the process of decaying, we will take it to Malacca."

The grave was opened and the coffin brought up. When the lid was removed, the diggers fell back in amazement. The body of Saint Francis Xavier was exactly as it had been when he had died! No decay had set it, nor had the lime harmed the flesh. The sailors blessed themselves, sealed the coffin again, and took it out to the ship.

Malacca was reached late in March. The greatest procession the city had ever seen turned out to escort the body to the church where Saint Francis had so often preached. Only a few people were missing from the procession—the wicked captain who had prevented the journey to China and some of his close friends. This evil man, who was so soon to have leprosy, is said to have played checkers as the procession went past him.

The body was buried once again, this time with no coffin. For five months it lay in the ground. Then a close friend of Saint Francis arrived in Malacca and asked to see the remains. Once again it was dug up. Again it was discovered that no decay had taken place. The body was as fresh as at the moment of death. The friends of Saint Francis decided that such a treasure should be taken to Goa, the largest Portuguese center in the Orient.

The body was taken to the home of the trader who had been made Francis' ambassador to China. Here it was wrapped in rich cloth which had been bought as a present for the Chinese emperor. Not until December did a ship sail for India, so Saint Francis was well over a year dead when his perfectly preserved body reached Goa.

Once again an entire city turned out to honor the memory of the missioner. Never before or since was there anything like the sadness which swept over Goa. The Dominican priest who preached at the funeral could not be heard for the sobbing in the huge cathedral. Finally, his own tears forced him to leave the pulpit.

A Jesuit who had known Saint Francis Xavier has left us a description of the body as it appeared almost a year and a half after death. This is what he wrote: "He looked exactly as we remembered him, lying there in his priestly robes as if he had died only a half hour ago. Under the vestments, next to the skin, the body was clothed in a rich robe which the Father had taken with him from Goa to wear for his meeting with the emperor of China. Though it had been more than a year under the earth, it was so clean and fresh that Father Nunes was able to wear it later when he paid visits to the kings of Japan."

Doctors were called to examine the body of the saint and to find out whether or not it had been embalmed. The doctors examined the body carefully and declared that it had not been preserved by "any natural or artificial means." There was no other conclusion but that God had worked a great miracle in behalf of Saint Francis Xavier.

For four days, from dawn until midnight, crowds passed through the cathedral to see the body and kiss the feet of the saint who had journeyed so far for God. Then the body was placed in a special shrine especially built for it. From time to time the shrine was opened, and the body shown to the people. But each time the appearance of the body caused so much excitement among the people that the officials thought it best that the tomb be closed again.

One hundred and forty years after the body was placed in the tomb, it was brought out so that an important bishop might see it. Present on that day was a French Jesuit. He writes that the body was in a perfect state, and he also gives a good description of Saint Francis Xavier.

"The Saint's hair is black and slightly curling," he wrote. "The forehead is broad and high, with two rather large veins, soft and of a purple tint, running down the middle, as is often seen in talented persons who spend much time in deep thought. The eyes are black, lively, and sweet, with so keen a glance that he would seem to be alive and breathing. The lips are of a warm reddish color and the beard is thick.

"In the cheeks there is a pale pink tint. The tongue is quite flexible, red, and moist, and the chin is beautifully shaped. In a word the body has all the appearances of a living man. It is so great a marvel, that on seeing it, while I was present, the Commissioner of the Dutch East India Company became at once a convert to the Catholic Faith."

Not long after this, the body began to darken and dry up. When it was photographed in 1932, it had become mummified.

The fact that the body is now mummified does not lessen the miracle of its preservation for a hundred and fifty years. A miracle does not have to last forever to be a miracle. When Our Lord brought to life the dead son of the widow of Naim, that young man died again some years later. But that does not make the miracle any less important.

God showed his love of Saint Francis Xavier in many other miracles both during the lifetime of the saint and after his death.

On March 12, 1622, Francis Xavier, along with his spiritual father, Ignatius Loyola, was canonized and declared to be a saint. Later he was named the patron of all foreign missions of the Catholic Church.

Today throughout the world Saint Francis Xavier is held in great esteem, not only by Catholics, but also by people who are not Christians. His shrine in Goa draws great crowds every year. Another shrine was built on Sancian Island at the spot where he died.

Saint Francis Xavier's influence did not end with his death. Because of his influence a vast army of missioners—priests, Brothers and Sisters—have gone to distant parts of the world to teach men about God. They work today in great numbers in the very lands where Francis spent his priestly life. Many of them face dangers and hardships like the ones that he faced. Many of them will die far from families and friends, just as he died.

But dangers and hardships will not keep young Americans from going to help their fellow men. Like Saint Francis Xavier they believe that the command Christ gave His Church to "go and teach all nations" was meant for them. Like Saint Francis Xavier they burn with a heavenly fire that would consume all men. Yet their numbers are pitifully small and the world so vast! With Saint Francis Xavier they pray for more helpers to preach Christ's words to the world.

Saint Francis Xavier is their model. His passion for the souls of men becomes their meat and drink. His ardor to set the world afire with the love of God becomes their very lives. And just as Saint Francis Xavier walked in the footsteps of Christ seeking out those who were lost, so too these apostles of our own day go down the lanes and byways of the world yearning for the salvation of all mankind.